weekend

cooking

whitecap

First English edition by Whitecap Books
First published in French in 2005 by Les Éditions La Presse

Visit our website at www.whitecap.ca.

Translated by Anne-Marie Haché, Experience Communications
Edited by Andrew Tzembelicos
Proofread by Ben D'Andrea
Cover and interior design by Luz design + communications
Typeset by Jacqui Thomas and Five Seventeen

Printed and bound in Canada by Friesens

LIBRARY AND ARCHIVES CANADA CATALOGUING IN PUBLICATION

Larrivée, Ricardo
    Weekend cooking / Ricardo Larrivée.

Includes index.
Translation of: Ma cuisine week-end.
ISBN 1-55285-787-5

    1. Cookery. I. Title.

TX714.L36613 2006   641.5   C2005-906780-2

The publisher acknowledges the financial support of the
Government of Canada through the Book Publishing Industry
Development Program for our publishing activities.

Contents

To the loves of my life:
Brigitte, Béatrice, Clémence and Jeanne

Preface

My only aim in cooking is enjoyment! The enjoyment of sharing, of tasting, of touching foods that will become small wonders or major events. For as long as I can remember, I've always loved standing behind the kitchen counter with flour-covered hands. The movements involved in cooking make me happy; its creative silence calms me. I love to cook, not only to discover flavours but also to reap the satisfaction of offering food to those I love.

I really enjoyed creating this book and especially getting people to taste the many different recipe versions. I got everyone in the family involved. I don't know how many times a day I called upon Pierrette, my mother-in-law, for her input on a salad dressing or a cake. I must tell you that Pierrette spends weekdays at our house taking care of our daughters. Without her love and support, there's no way we could enjoy all the extraordinary things happening in our lives right now. I can hear you say, "What a lucky woman! She gets to eat all the time!" In fact, it's not that easy to go from tasting a marinade to a piece of pie, trying out a beef dish, and then a piece of fudge, with the kids running around, friends stopping by, and her son-in-law agonizing over his latest recipe! I assure you, our Pierrette is a tower of strength.

Over the past few years on my television show,* I've attempted to answer the question we all ask when opening the fridge each and every day, "What can I make?" After running around all week, we cherish the weekend. Cooking then takes on a whole new life.

From a stress-filled activity for many, it becomes the perfect excuse for some much-deserved relaxation.

By offering easy-to-make recipes, I want to help you focus on atmosphere. I thought of what I love to do on weekends: watch a movie with my buddies, have brunch with the family, welcome friends over or organize a party for the kids. Unlike weekdays, there's time for a more ambitious menu.

I also thought about wine. How many of us face rows of bottles at the liquor store, hoping for some inspiration? Matching a wine with the right dish can really enhance the pleasure of a meal. With this in mind, I called upon the talent of sommelier Alain Bélanger.

I see this book as a pretext for celebration. The beauty of cooking is that there are no limits. People can experiment with the recipes. This is, at the very least, what I wish for.

* Translator's Note: program presented daily by the Société Radio-Canada, CBC's French counterpart

Merci !

If I had to choose just one person to thank, it would be you my darling Brigitte, for everything you've brought into my life. Without you, happiness wouldn't have been possible, my ambitions would have been in vain. Because of you, our three daughters blossom more and more every day. You're an amazing mother! The opportunity to work with your great talent is an incredible gift, and living with you is an unbelievable privilege.

Together, we've decided to make cooking an activity we can re-invent every day. Because of your legendary sense of organization, your rigorous intellect and tireless determination, you've succeeded in channelling my boundless energy.

This is my first book and a dream come true. Although I may work in the kitchen alone, it's the desire to sit at the table with family and friends that inspires me. Sharing is the essence of cooking. I share this book with all who love to cook and those who have contributed their special gifts to make it possible.

Thank you, Nathaly Simard, with whom I cook, taste and taste again on an almost daily basis. What wonderful recipes we've concocted.

I owe this beautiful book, in large part, to Christian Lacroix and his team. I still have to pinch myself when I think of how lucky I am to work with you. Thank you, Christian, for your generosity, your sensitivity and your immense creativity evident in every picture. To see my cooking come alive through your lens is pure magic.

Christian isn't alone in the studio. In recent years, I've also fallen under the spell of Lise Carrière and Anne Gagné. Lise, I must tell you, over and above your design, it's your hugs, worthy of an Olympic goddess, that always make me feel special. Your good taste is nothing short of perfection. Anne, with her nimble fingers, has so much talent: she can turn a meatball stew into a visual masterpiece. Thanks to both of you. Pierre-Luc, you complete this incredible team. Because of you, glasses are full, and so are the rolls of film. Thanks also to you, Lise Madore, Christian's guardian angel, and ours as well.

Lucie Arsenault, you're amazing. I know of few artistic directors as patient and dedicated as you. You worked on this book as if it were your own. Up until the very last minute, you added all the finishing touches, making it a source of pride for us all. Thanks also to your team: Ghislaine Tremblay, Patrick Sirois, Élise Bergeron and Denis Rainville.

Thank you, Hélène Paquet and Frédérique Laliberté, for your language skills. Thank you, Alain Bélanger, not only for your wine suggestions but also for making wine a pleasure that's accessible to all, something you do without any snobbishness whatsoever.

Many thanks to the whole team at Whitecap Books for offering me this opportunity to share my passion with the rest of the country. Because of you, I've been able to fulfill a long-held dream. In this day and age, it's a privilege to work with people who pride themselves on quality over quantity. Special thanks and my fondest regards to you, Robert McCullough, for your trust in me and your contagious enthusiasm.

Many thanks also to my mum, my first taster, for having made me what I am (against all odds). I thank you for passing on your sense of family and your boundless optimism. To you, Martine, my dear sister, who tasted my first recipes, I promise . . . I'll make meringues for you when we both retire to an old-age home!

Last of all, thank you, my dear readers, for your faithfulness.

Before getting started

Here's some information on the equipment, ingredients and techniques I use to create my recipes.

Little things can make all the difference between a heavy cake and a light one, baked to perfection.

EQUIPMENT

OVEN
All recipes have been tested in a conventional oven. Cooking times are for preheated ovens. Oven thermostats aren't always accurate and may vary. Check the accuracy of your oven thermostat with an oven thermometer and adjust if necessary. If you're using a convection oven, lower the cooking temperature for your recipes by 25°F / 15°C and the cooking time by 25 percent.

MEAT THERMOMETER
When roasting meat or whole chicken, I indicate approximate cooking times, but nothing is more accurate than checking the internal temperature of the meat with a meat thermometer.

PANS AND COOKIE SHEETS
I use pans and sheets made of aluminum, with a matte finish. If yours are black or very dark, reduce the cooking time by a few minutes. Increase the cooking time if they're very shiny.

PAN SIZE
I always specify which pan size to use. To verify the size of your pans, measure them from the inside, not including the rim.

INGREDIENTS

EGGS
Recipes have been tested using large eggs.

BUTTER
I use salted butter unless otherwise specified.

ALL-PURPOSE FLOUR
Recipes call for all-purpose flour, unless otherwise specified. (I prefer unbleached all-purpose flour.)

PASTRY FLOUR
Most of the time, I use this type of flour for cakes. This is specified for you in the recipes.

MEASURING TECHNIQUES

FLOUR
All-purpose flour isn't sifted before being measured. I use the following technique for measuring flour: with the help of a spoon, put the flour in a straight-edged measuring cup. Overfill and level with a knife. Don't dip the cup directly into the flour bag or shake or hit the cup; you could add up to 2 to 3 Tbsp (25 to 45 mL) more flour! This will weigh down any recipe.

BROWN SUGAR
Brown sugar is measured by pressing it down lightly in the measuring cup.

LIQUIDS
Liquids are measured in a Pyrex-type measuring cup with a spout.

early mornings
with family

Brunches and Breakfasts

My daughters adore eating eggs served in eggcups. According to them, it's much more fun than eating scrambled eggs. To make it even more exciting, I add *fleur de sel** onto the runny yolk, and then we dip bread sticks garnished with cheese and bacon into the yolks. Bread sticks with an attitude!

Boiled Eggs, Revisited

PREPARATION TIME
10 MINUTES

COOKING TIME
10 MINUTES

SERVES
4

8 slices bacon, finely chopped
½ cup (125 mL) old cheddar, grated
2 tsp (10 mL) fresh chives, minced
ground pepper
4 slices of white crusty bread,
     without crust
4 eggs

Place rack on upper shelf of oven. Preheat to Broil.

In skillet, fry bacon until crispy. Drain using paper towels.

In bowl, mix bacon, cheese, chives and pepper.

Toast bread in oven for a few minutes. Spread bacon mix on grilled bread. Set aside.

Delicately place eggs in pot of boiling water. Let boil for 4 minutes, until medium-cooked (eggs will be firm and white, with runny yolk).

Meanwhile, under broiler, grill bread slices, garnished with cheese and bacon, until cheese has melted.

Cut each slice of bread into 4 strips, which will serve as bread sticks for the eggs.

Place eggs in eggcups. Cut tops off with a knife or egg slicer. Serve with bread sticks, which can be dipped into egg yolk.

*Salt with a distinct taste and fragrance, gathered in a thin layer on the surface of salt pans.

One beautiful Sunday, I visited my friend Jean-Paul and his wife Sylvie at their home for lunch. The menu consisted of potato cakes, better known as rösti. We ate tons of them! Jean-Paul is Alsatian and, oh, what a cook! He takes great delight in criticizing my European recipes; thankfully, his wife usually takes my side. Here's my version of this Swiss dish. (I can't wait for your comments, Jean-Paul!)

Smoked Trout Rösti
with lime-flavoured sour cream

PREPARATION TIME
15 MINUTES

COOKING TIME
40 MINUTES

SERVES
4

3 parsnips, peeled and grated
2 potatoes, peeled and grated
6 Tbsp (90 mL) butter
⅓ cup (75 mL) sour cream
1 Tbsp (15 mL) lime juice
2 Tbsp (25 mL) fresh chives, minced
Tabasco sauce, to taste
salt and pepper
¼ lb (125 g) smoked trout or any
*   other smoked fish, thinly sliced*
chives for decoration

In bowl, mix parsnips and potatoes, for a total of 4 cups (1 L) of vegetables. Season with salt and pepper.

Divide vegetables into 4 even parts. In a non-stick skillet, melt half of the butter over low-medium heat. Add 2 parts vegetables, shaping them into 5-inch (12-cm) circles. Brown for 10 minutes, flattening well with spatula. Flip over carefully and brown for another 10 minutes.

Transfer cooked rösti to plate or serving dish and keep warm. Cook remaining rösti in remaining butter.

In a small bowl, mix sour cream, lime juice, chives and Tabasco. Season with salt and pepper.

Place each rösti on a plate. Add a little flavoured sour cream and a few slices of smoked fish to each. Decorate with chives, and season with salt and pepper. Serve.

A perfect dish for brunch.

A LITTLE WINE?
Accompany rösti with
a nice white, such as a
Bordeaux or Graves.

Banana Bread

2 cups (500 mL) pastry flour
2 tsp (10 mL) baking powder
½ cup (125 mL) unsalted butter,
    softened
1 cup (250 mL) brown sugar,
    slightly compacted
2 eggs, beaten
1 tsp (5 mL) vanilla extract
1¼ cups (300 mL) bananas
    (about 3), mashed
½ cup (125 mL) milk

Place rack in the centre of oven. Preheat to 350°F (180°C). Grease a 9- × 5-inch (23- × 13-cm) loaf pan with butter.

In a bowl, mix flour and baking powder. Set aside.

In another bowl, beat butter and brown sugar for 1 minute, until mixture lightens in colour.

Add eggs and vanilla to the butter and sugar mixture and beat until eggs and vanilla are well incorporated. Add mashed banana and stir with wooden spoon. Add dry ingredients and milk, alternating.

Spread bread dough in loaf pan. Bake in oven for approximately 1 hour, or until a toothpick inserted in the centre comes out clean.

Cool before turning out and slicing.

Variation: For banana and nut bread add 1 cup (250 mL) of chopped nuts to the recipe. Add the nuts to the mixture at the same time as the mashed bananas.

Waffles
with cinnamon apple sauce

Cinnamon Apple Sauce

3 Tbsp (45 mL) butter
3 McIntosh apples, peeled, seeded and sliced
3 Cortland apples, peeled, seeded and sliced
¼ cup (50 mL) sugar
1 tsp (5 mL) ground cinnamon
1 Tbsp (15 mL) cornstarch
1 cup (250 mL) apple juice

Waffles

2 cups (500 mL) pastry flour
2 tsp (10 mL) baking powder
¼ cup (50 mL) sugar
1¼ cups (300 mL) milk
1 tsp (5 mL) vanilla extract
3 eggs, separated
¼ cup (50 mL) unsalted butter, melted and cooled

Cinnamon Apple Sauce

In saucepan, melt butter. Add apples and fry quickly for 2 minutes over high heat. Add sugar and cinnamon. Cook over medium heat for about 10 minutes.

Mix cornstarch with apple juice. Add to apple mixture and stir until boiling. Set aside.

Waffles

In a bowl, mix flour, baking powder and sugar. In another bowl, mix milk, vanilla and egg yolks. In a third bowl, beat egg whites until firm peaks form. Set aside.

Using a wooden spoon, add milk mixture to dry ingredients. Fold in egg whites and then butter.

Pour part of batter into a waffle iron. Cook for about 6 minutes, or until waffles are golden.

Top waffles with apple sauce and serve.

I used to go to the mall when I was young, and I was irresistibly captivated by the aroma of cinnamon buns. A bit like Obélix, who followed the boar's scent, my nose always led me to the counter where they sold hot pecan buns . . . and I fell for them each and every time! It was to enjoy this small pleasure at home that I created this recipe.

Caramel and Pecan Buns

PREPARATION TIME
20 MINUTES

RISING TIME
2 HOURS, 15 MINUTES

COOKING TIME
25 MINUTES

MAKES
18 BUNS

4 cups + 2 Tbsp (1 L + 25 mL) flour
2 tsp (10 mL) fast-rising yeast
    or 1 envelope
2 Tbsp (25 mL) sugar
1 tsp (5 mL) salt
½ cup (125 mL) unsalted butter,
    softened
2 eggs
1¼ cups (300 mL) milk, lukewarm

Filling
1 Tbsp (15 mL) melted butter
½ cup (125 mL) brown sugar
1 tsp (5 mL) ground cinnamon

Icing
¼ cup (50 mL) butter
¼ cup (50 mL) corn syrup
½ cup (125 mL) brown sugar
2 Tbsp (25 mL) water
1 cup (250 mL) whole roasted pecans

In bowl, mix dry ingredients. Add butter, eggs and milk. Combine, kneading until a ball forms. Knead dough for another 5 minutes with hands or with pastry hook of an electric mixer.

Place dough in a large greased bowl. Cover with clean cloth and let rise in a warm place (like a microwave oven in which a glass of hot water has been placed) for 45 minutes.

Filling
Liberally sprinkle flour over working area, dough and rolling pin. Then roll out dough to obtain a 20- × 14-inch (50- × 35-cm) rectangle. Brush with melted butter.

In a bowl, mix brown sugar and cinnamon and sprinkle onto dough. Roll dough firmly, like a cake roll, into 20-inch (50-cm) long roll.

Cut roll into 18 slices. Put slices in 15- × 10-inch (38- × 25-cm) buttered Pyrex mould, but don't let slices touch sides. Cover with clean cloth. Let rise in a warm place for 1½ hours.

Place rack in centre of oven. Preheat to 350°F (180°C). Cook for about 25 minutes until buns are golden.

Icing
In a saucepan, heat butter, corn syrup, brown sugar and water.

When buns are ready, cover with pecans. Top with hot caramel and spread with brush if needed. Cool.

Ah! Vacation time! When I was a boy, we went back to the same place, in Naples, Maine, for years. Always the same people: my parents, sister and grandmother. I discovered my first American blueberry pancakes in the small village coffee shop. For me, this huge pile of pancakes (ordered in English by my French-speaking father) was fantastic.

Blueberry Pancakes

PREPARATION TIME
10 MINUTES

COOKING TIME
45 MINUTES

MAKES
12 PANCAKES

2 cups (500 mL) flour
2 tsp (10 mL) baking powder
¼ cup (50 mL) sugar
2 eggs
2 cups (500 mL) milk
1 tsp (5 mL) vanilla extract
*1¼ cups (300 mL) fresh or thawed
    blueberries*
butter
maple syrup to serve

In a bowl, mix flour and baking powder. Add remaining ingredients, except blueberries. Beat mixture until all ingredients are well mixed.

If blueberries are fresh, gently add to batter. If using frozen berries, add thawed berries to skillet when the pancakes are cooking.

In a non-stick skillet, melt a little butter. Pour about ¼ cup (50 mL) of batter into skillet. Spread batter out by moving skillet to form pancake of about 6 inches (15 cm) in diameter. If using thawed berries, top pancakes with 1 Tbsp (15 mL).

Cook pancakes for about 2 minutes per side. Set aside and keep warm.

Drizzle maple syrup over pancakes and serve.

French toast is an unavoidable breakfast tradition. One day, I was looking for a way to update this standard dish. Our photographer, Christian Lacroix, remembered a crunchy California version. Coated with muesli, this weekend classic takes on a new dimension. Christian, there's a little of you in this recipe.

Crunchy French Toast
and crème anglaise (French vanilla sauce)

PREPARATION TIME
15 MINUTES

COOKING TIME
30 MINUTES

SERVES
4

Crème Anglaise

6 egg yolks
½ cup (125 mL) sugar
2½ cups (625 mL) milk, warm
½ vanilla bean, cut in half, or
  1 tsp (5 mL) vanilla extract

French Toast

3 eggs, beaten
2 cups (500 mL) milk
½ cup (125 mL) maple syrup
3½ cups (875 mL) muesli,
  without raisins
⅓ cup (75 mL) unsalted butter
8 slices of homemade bread
fresh fruit, for garnish

Crème Anglaise

In upper part of a double boiler, before heating, beat egg yolks and sugar until colour lightens. Add milk. With tip of a knife, scrape out inside of vanilla bean. Add seeds and bean to mixture. (If you don't have a vanilla bean, use vanilla extract.)

Over a saucepan of simmering water (water shouldn't touch upper part of double boiler), cook mixture for about 10 minutes, stirring constantly with wooden spoon, until mixture completely coats back of spoon. Remove from double boiler and cool. Discard vanilla bean. Cover crème anglaise with plastic wrap and refrigerate.

French Toast

In a bowl, beat eggs, milk and maple syrup. Pulse muesli in food processor, or put in bag and crush with rolling pin.

In a medium-sized skillet, heat butter. Dip bread slices into egg batter to drench them, then coat with muesli.

In the hot skillet, brown bread slices on both sides. Before serving, top French toast with cold crème anglaise or maple syrup and garnish with fresh fruit.

Ricotta-Stuffed Pancakes
with orange sauce

Pancakes

1 egg
2 Tbsp (30 mL) sugar
1 tsp (5 mL) vanilla extract
1 cup (250 mL) flour
1½ cups (375 mL) milk
butter

Stuffing

2 cups (500 mL) ricotta cheese
*   (or one 475-g container)*
¼ cup (50 mL) sugar
1 tsp (5 mL) vanilla extract
zest of 1 orange
½ cup (125 mL) whipped
*   cream (optional)*

Orange Sauce

3 navel oranges
2 Tbsp (30 mL) cornstarch
1 cup (250 mL) orange juice
2 Tbsp (30 mL) sugar
6 Tbsp (90 mL) Grand Marnier
*   or other orange liqueur*

Pancakes

In a bowl, beat egg, sugar and vanilla. Add flour and milk, alternating, mixing until smooth and all ingredients have been incorporated.

Lightly butter a non-stick skillet. Cook pancakes, in batches, in hot skillet, browning on both sides. Pile onto plate and cover with plastic wrap.

Stuffing

In a bowl, mix cheese, sugar, vanilla and orange zest. Add whipped cream, if desired. Stuff pancakes with this mix. Set aside.

Orange Sauce

Quick-peel oranges.* In a bowl, mix cornstarch with juice. In saucepan, melt sugar until lightly golden. Deglaze with orange liqueur; mixture will harden. Combine juice and cornstarch, and add to saucepan. Cook over low heat, stirring until sauce thickens. Add orange segments, stirring lightly to reheat.

Top pancakes, either lukewarm or cold, with the hot orange sauce. Serve immediately.

*To quick-peel an orange: Place orange on cutting board. Using well-sharpened knife, cut orange at both ends. Then remove rind, cutting as close as possible to the flesh. Once rind has been removed, cut orange into segments, taking care to make cuts between fruit and membrane on each side. Lift out each segment and set aside. Work over a bowl to collect juice.

Eggs Benedict

PREPARATION TIME
15 MINUTES

COOKING TIME
20 MINUTES

SERVES
2 TO 4

Hollandaise Sauce

2 egg yolks
2 Tbsp (25 mL) lemon or
  clementine juice
½ cup (125 mL) cold butter, cubed
salt and pepper

Eggs

2 tsp (10 mL) white vinegar
2 to 4 eggs
1 to 2 English muffins
2 to 4 healthy slices of black forest
  ham, at room temperature

Hollandaise Sauce

In the upper part of a double boiler, before heating, beat yolks and lemon juice. Place upper part of double boiler over simmering (not boiling) water.

Beat egg and lemon mixture until hot and fluffy. Add butter, one cube at a time. Beat after each addition until butter has melted. Texture will gradually thicken. Taste and season, if necessary. Keep sauce over lukewarm water while poaching eggs.

Eggs

In a large saucepan, bring water and vinegar to a simmer. Break eggs into saucers. Slide 2 eggs at a time into water and poach for about 3 minutes, or until cooked to your taste. Normally, yolks should be runny. Place poached eggs on paper towels to drain, taking care not to break yolks. Repeat with remaining eggs.

While eggs are poaching, cut and toast English muffins. Place one slice of ham and one egg on each half. If need be, keep warm in preheated oven (150°F / 75°C) for a few minutes.

Top with hollandaise sauce and serve.

Hot Chocolate
and homemade marshmallow

PREPARATION TIME
30 MINUTES

WAITING TIME
OVERNIGHT

COOKING TIME
10 MINUTES

SERVES
4

Hot Chocolate

4 cups (1 L) milk
1 tsp (5 mL) vanilla extract
6 oz (175 g) fine bittersweet or
*   milk chocolate, chopped*

Homemade Marshmallow

canola or corn oil
1½ cups (375 mL) sugar
⅓ cup (75 mL) hot water
1 tsp (5 mL) vanilla extract
5 tsp (25 mL) gelatin
½ cup (125 mL) cold water
3 Tbsp (40 mL) icing sugar
1 Tbsp (15 mL) cornstarch

Hot Chocolate

In a medium saucepan, heat milk and vanilla. Add chocolate, stirring so chocolate melts. Beat hot chocolate, topping with marshmallow before serving.

Homemade Marshmallow

Cover the bottom of a 9- × 13-inch (23- × 33-cm) pan with plastic wrap and oil well using hands. It's important to oil pan completely.

In bowl, mix sugar and water. Add vanilla.

In another bowl, let gelatin expand in cold water for about 2 to 3 minutes, then dissolve completely using microwave oven or double boiler on stovetop. Add gelatin to sugar mixture.

Beat sugar mixture with electric mixer for about 10 minutes or until mixture has soft meringue texture. Spread in pan. Let set, overnight, at room temperature.

After mixture has set, cut marshmallow into cubes. Roll cubes in mixture of icing sugar and cornstarch.

working up
an appetite

Hors d'Oeuvres, Soups and Appetizers

FLAVOURS TINTED WITH A WARM SUN. A SPARKLING AND UPLIFTING TASTE. HERE ARE THREE COCKTAILS THAT WILL MAKE EVERYONE SMILE.

Weekend Cocktails

Sunny Girl

ice cubes
1 Tbsp (15 mL) Campari
1 Tbsp (15 mL) dark rum
½ cup (125 mL) tangerine
  juice, approximately
slice of orange, for garnish

Pour all ingredients into a highball glass filled wih ice cubes. Decorate with a slice of orange. Serve.

Cuban Lemonade

2 Tbsp (25 mL) white rum
1 Tbsp (15 mL) peach schnapps
½ cup (125 mL) lemonade,
  approximately
crushed ice

Pour all ingredients into a highball glass; add ice. Mix and serve.

Blush

¼ cup (50 mL) white wine
¼ cup (50 mL) cranberry juice
¼ cup (50 mL) apple juice
1 Tbsp (15 mL) vodka
1 tsp (5 mL) Cointreau or
  other orange liqueur
ice cubes
peach wedge or cranberries,
  for decoration

Pour all ingredients into an old-fashioned glass. Mix and decorate with peach or fresh cranberries. Serve.

Tapas
Marinated Eggplant, Chorizos and Watermelon with Goat Cheese

Tapas are to Spaniards what antipasti are to Italians: simple dishes savoured at cocktail time or as an appetizer. Tapas can be part of a buffet, or the whole meal. On the weekend, I love serving tapas when entertaining friends, without any fuss. Among the classics are spicy chorizo sausage, goat cheese in olive oil, olives, clams and other seafood. I also like preparing bite-sized treats rooted in Spanish culinary tradition but "revamped" with a modern touch, such as my Watermelon with Goat Cheese.

Marinated Eggplants

PREPARATION TIME
10 MINUTES

COOKING TIME
55 MINUTES

SERVES
6 TO 8

¼ cup (50 mL) olive oil
8 garlic cloves, peeled and cut in half
½ sprig fresh rosemary
1 sweet yellow pepper,
    cut into 16 cubes
1 sweet red pepper, cut into 16 cubes
salt and pepper
4 small Italian eggplants,
    6 oz (175 g) each
¾ cup (175 mL) balsamic vinegar
6 cups (1.5 L) water
2 sprigs fresh thyme
3 bay leaves

In small saucepan, heat olive oil. Add garlic and rosemary. Cook over low heat for about 10 minutes. Add peppers and continue cooking for another 5 minutes. Season with salt and pepper. Drain using a colander, reserving peppers, oil and garlic.

Place the whole eggplants into a casserole dish. Add reserved peppers and garlic, balsamic vinegar, water, thyme and bay leaves. Season with salt and pepper. Bring to a boil, reduce heat and simmer for 40 minutes. Drain through a colander, discarding liquid, thyme, garlic and bay leaves. Cool.

Cut eggplants in half lengthwise, then into medium-sized pieces. Place in bowl with peppers. Drizzle reserved oil over the top. Season with salt and pepper. Cool. Serve as appetizers at room temperature. Keep leftovers refrigerated.

Chorizos

PREPARATION TIME
5 MINUTES

COOKING TIME
10 MINUTES

SERVES
4 TO 6

1 Tbsp (15 mL) olive oil
1 lb (560 g) chorizos
(Portuguese sausages) cut
into ½-inch (1-cm) slices
1 tsp (5 mL) fennel seeds
½ cup (125 mL) white wine

In medium skillet, heat olive oil. Add sausages and brown for about 2 minutes on each side over medium heat. Add fennel seeds and then deglaze with white wine.

Simmer slowly until all liquid has evaporated. Serve sausages lukewarm, with toothpicks.

Watermelon with Goat Cheese

PREPARATION TIME
15 MINUTES

COOKING TIME
10 MINUTES

MAKES
30 BITE-SIZED APPETIZERS

2 Tbsp (25 mL) olive oil
3 garlic cloves, peeled and cut in half
3 slices bacon, finely chopped
1 roll (3⅓ oz / 100 g) soft unripened
goat cheese, crumbled
2 Tbsp (25 mL) fresh chervil, minced
30 cubes watermelon, ½ inch (1.5
cm) wide by 1 inch (2.5 cm) high
pepper
chervil leaves, to decorate

In small skillet, heat olive oil. Add garlic and cook for approximately 5 minutes. Set aside oil and discard garlic.

In another skillet, cook bacon until crispy. Drain using paper towel to absorb excess fat. Set aside.

In a small bowl, mix crumbled cheese, garlic-flavoured oil, bacon and chervil. Season with pepper.

On each cube of watermelon, place about 1 tsp (5 mL) of the cheese and bacon mix. Garnish with chervil leaf and serve.

WHAT TO DRINK?

With tapas, we drink sherry, of course! Try a Fino or Montilla-Morilles Fino for an authentic Spanish touch.

There are many stories about the origins of tapas. One that amuses me explains that in Andalusia (in southern Spain), people would eat outside and drink sherry, which attracts insects with its fragrance. To protect the contents of their glasses, someone had the brilliant idea of putting a little cover on top, which resembled a small saucer called a tapa. In restaurants, waiters started to serve a few olives, a piece of sausage or other bite-sized appetizers on the tapa, which gave its name to the famous hors d'oeuvres.

Spinach Phyllo Bites

PREPARATION TIME
15 MINUTES

COOKING TIME
10 MINUTES

MAKES
12 BITE-SIZED APPETIZERS

1 green onion, finely chopped
3 garlic cloves, chopped
2 Tbsp (25 mL) olive oil
7 oz (200 g) lean ground beef
½ tsp (2 mL) dried oregano
salt and pepper
2 cups (500 mL) fresh
*   spinach, chopped*
6 Tbsp (90 mL) feta cheese, crumbled
1 egg
6 phyllo sheets
¼ cup (50 mL) butter, melted

Place rack in centre of oven. Preheat oven to 350°F (180°C). Cover bottom of cookie sheet with parchment paper.

In a medium saucepan, soften onion and garlic in oil. Add beef and oregano, cooking over high heat. With a wooden spoon, break down meat until fully cooked. Season with salt and pepper.

Add spinach to the saucepan and cook until wilted. Remove from heat and cool. Add cheese and egg. Mix well. Season to taste.

On a smooth work surface, lay down a phyllo sheet. Brush phyllo sheet with melted butter. Cover with two other sheets, also brushed with melted butter. Cut into 12 squares. Place 1 Tbsp (15 mL) beef mixture into the middle of each square. Fold two corners, perpendicular to filling, towards the centre. Fold the other two corners, then roll to form a small phyllo bite. Brush with butter.

Place rolls on cookie sheet. Bake in oven for about 10 minutes. Serve as appetizers.

AS FOR WINE?
A medium-bodied red wine from Greece.

I must confess: I'm about as sports-oriented as a squirrel. (Even then, I'm not so sure.) While I did manage to catch a few footballs in college, food was always my main goal. Exhausted and aching all over, the reward was worth the effort. The cold beer, nachos, chicken wings, fried zucchinis and potato jackets brought me back to life. Weekend evenings, in front of a hockey game, the Super Bowl or a good movie, the footstool is the perfect table for this "fine dining." Here are two recipes to bring a sporty atmosphere to your living room.

Mozzarella Sticks

PREPARATION TIME
10 MINUTES

COOKING TIME
5 MINUTES

MAKES
4

½ cup (125 mL) flour
½ cup (125 mL) Italian bread crumbs
1 egg
½ lb (250 g) mozzarella, cut into sticks
    ½ inch (1 cm) by 3 inches (7.5 cm)
2 Tbsp (25 mL) olive oil

Put flour in one bowl and bread crumbs in another.

In a small bowl, beat egg.

Dredge the cheese sticks in flour. Dip them into the egg and coat with bread crumbs. If desired, place sticks in freezer for 30 minutes for easier handling when cooking.

In large skillet, brown cheese sticks in oil over medium-high heat. Serve hot or lukewarm.

Cajun-Style Chicken Wings

PREPARATION TIME
15 MINUTES

MARINATING TIME
2 TO 24 HOURS

COOKING TIME
45 MINUTES

MAKES
48 WINGS

24 chicken wings
¾ cup (175 mL) ketchup
2 Tbsp (25 mL) brown sugar
2 Tbsp (25 mL) chili powder
1 tsp (5 mL) ground cumin
2 tsp (10 mL) dried thyme
2 tsp (10 mL) garlic salt
1½ tsp (75 mL) Tabasco sauce,
    or to taste

Place rack on bottom level of oven.
Preheat oven to 375°F (190°C).

Notice that the wings have two joints. With chef's knife, cut each joint (yielding 3 pieces per wing). Throw out the pointed end with no meat. You should have 48 pieces.

Mix remaining ingredients in a bowl. Add chicken and marinate from 2 to 24 hours in refrigerator.

Cover cookie sheet with parchment paper. Place wings and cook in oven for about 45 minutes.

Grilled Scallops
on basil-flavoured whipped cream

PREPARATION TIME
20 MINUTES

WAITING TIME
4 HOURS

COOKING TIME
20 MINUTES

MAKES
30 APPETIZERS

1 cup (250 mL) 35% whipping cream
1 cup (250 mL) fresh basil, minced
Tabasco, to taste
30 small scallops, trimmed
1 Tbsp (15 mL) vegetable oil
2 Tbsp (25 mL) butter
Salt and pepper
Fresh chives
Pink peppercorns, to decorate

In a small saucepan, bring cream to a boil. Remove from heat. Add basil, stir and cool. Refrigerate for 4 hours.

Pass cold basil cream through sieve. Beat until peaks form. Season with Tabasco sauce, to taste.

In a medium skillet, brown scallops in oil and butter. Season with salt and pepper.

To serve, place about 2 tsp (5 mL) of whipped cream into a silver soup spoon. Top with a lukewarm scallop. Decorate with chives and one peppercorn.

Don't forget to remove the small muscle that attaches the scallop to its shell.

WHAT TO DRINK?
Good wine,
such as a
Blanquette
de Limoux

39

Sweet Potato Soup
with apples and cloves

PREPARATION TIME
15 MINUTES

COOKING TIME
25 MINUTES

SERVES
6

1 leek, white part only, chopped
3 Tbsp (40 mL) butter
1 apple, peeled, cored and
    cut into pieces
3 medium sweet potatoes,
    peeled and cut into pieces
¼ cup (50 mL) white wine or
    chicken stock
5 cups (1.25 L) chicken stock
⅛ tsp (0.5 mL) ground clove
salt and pepper
apple slices, to decorate

In medium saucepan, soften leek in butter. Add apples and sweet potatoes. Deglaze with white wine.

Add stock and clove. Cover and simmer until sweet potatoes are cooked, about 20 minutes.

Process in blender. Season with salt and pepper. Serve hot.

Decorate with slices of apple, fried quickly in butter, if desired.

Asian-Style Chicken Kebabs

PREPARATION TIME
15 MINUTES

MARINATING TIME
3 HOURS

COOKING TIME
6 MINUTES

MAKES
15 KEBABS

Marinade

½ cup (125 mL) vegetable oil
2 Tbsp (30 mL) lime juice
2 tsp (10 mL) soy sauce
1 tsp (5 mL) honey
1 garlic clove, finely chopped
1 tsp (5 mL) fresh ginger, chopped
Tabasco sauce, to taste
pepper

1¼ lb (600 g) chicken breasts, boned
    and skinned, cut into 15 strips
15 wooden skewers, soaked in
    water for 30 minutes
1 Tbsp (15 mL) black sesame seeds

Sauce

¼ cup (50 mL) soy sauce
¼ cup (50 mL) chicken stock
4 tsp (20 mL) honey
1 garlic clove, finely chopped
½ tsp (2 mL) fresh ginger, chopped

Marinade

Mix all ingredients in a bowl, seasoning with pepper. Add chicken. Cover and marinate in refrigerator for about 3 hours.

Sauce

Mix all ingredients in a bowl. Set aside in a cool place.

Place rack on top shelf of oven. Preheat to broil.

Thread chicken strips onto skewers. Place on cookie sheet and cook in oven for about 6 minutes.

Sprinkle with sesame seeds and serve with sauce.

WHAT TO DRINK?
A Pinot noir
from
California
or Oregon

Smoked Trout Blinis

PREPARATION TIME
10 MINUTES

WAITING TIME
1 HOUR, 10 MINUTES

COOKING TIME
20 MINUTES

MAKES
ABOUT 50 BLINIS

Blinis (Small Russian Pancakes)
1 cup (250 mL) milk, warm
½ tsp (2 mL) sugar
1 tsp (5 mL) fast-rising yeast
1¼ cups (300 mL) flour
2 Tbsp (25 mL) sour cream
3 Tbsp (40 mL) butter, melted
¼ cup (50 mL) fresh chives, minced
1 egg
Salt and pepper

Garnish
sour cream
smoked trout or salmon
fresh chives

In bowl, mix ¼ cup (50 mL) milk, sugar and yeast.
Let stand for 10 minutes at room temperature.

Add remaining milk and flour to mixture. Beat until well mixed. Cover with cloth or plastic wrap. Let stand for 1 hour at room temperature.

Mix sour cream, butter, chives and egg in a small bowl. Add to the above mixture. Season with salt and pepper.

In lightly buttered skillet, pour a little batter, forming small pancakes of about 2 inches (5 cm) in diameter. Cook remaining batter in the same manner. (If pancakes were prepared ahead of time and refrigerated, bring to room temperature before serving.)

Place a little sour cream on each blini. Garnish with smoked fish and chives.

Blinis can be prepared ahead of time and may even be frozen. Thaw them a day ahead of time, in the refrigerator, and serve them at room temperature.

AS FOR WINE?
A Canadian
or an Alsatian
Riesling

Not long ago, oyster parties were in vogue in the business world. Today, such cheerful events have almost disappeared due to the increased cost of seafood. It's unfortunate, since an oyster party is worth three golf games when it comes to negotiating a contract. Abraham Lincoln understood the value of oysters; during gargantuan feasts, he fed his voters nothing but oysters, prepared in every imaginable way. I don't know if they voted for him afterwards, but it was more fun than today's methods.

Five ways to serve
Oysters on the Shell

Exotic
*¼ cup (50 mL) mango, finely
    shredded*
2 Tbsp (25 mL) white wine vinegar
*1 Tbsp (15 mL) red sweet
    pepper, chopped*
1 pinch freshly ground pepper

Asian
3 Tbsp (40 mL) soy sauce
2 tsp (10 mL) fresh ginger, grated
1 green onion, finely chopped

Classic
raspberry vinegar
shallot, finely chopped

Italian
balsamic vinegar
dash of olive oil
one turn of pepper mill

My favourite
lime juice
Tabasco sauce, red or green

AS FOR WINE?
Nothing
beats
champagne.

Allow 6 oysters per person if served as an appetizer, or
about 2 dozen if served as the main course.

Grilled Dumplings
with satay sauce

PREPARATION TIME
1 HOUR

WAITING TIME
15 MINUTES

COOKING TIME
40 MINUTES

MAKES
60 DUMPLINGS

⅓ oz (10 g) dried shiitake mushrooms
4 boneless pork chops
2 green onions, finely chopped
2 garlic cloves, finely chopped
¼ cup (50 mL) water
*   chestnuts, chopped*
1 carrot, peeled and grated
1 Tbsp (15 mL) oyster sauce
¼ cup (50 mL) hoisin sauce
1 package (1 lb / 500 g) wonton
*   dough, thawed*
2 cups (500 mL) chicken stock
peanut oil
1 Tbsp (15 mL) non-toasted sesame oil
6 Tbsp (90 mL) crunchy peanut butter
hot pepper sauce, to taste
salt and pepper

Place mushrooms in bowl and cover with lukewarm water. Let stand about 15 minutes. Drain. Remove and discard stems, chop mushrooms and set aside.

Trim fat off pork chops, if necessary. Chop the trimmed meat into very small pieces.

Mix meat, green onions, garlic, water chestnuts, carrot, oyster sauce, hoisin sauce and mushrooms in medium-sized bowl.

Place 2 tsp (10 mL) of the mixture in the centre of each square of dough. Moisten sides of dough with water, and then fold to form a rectangle. Press sides to seal.

In saucepan, bring stock to boil. Poach dumplings, 6 at a time, for about 2 minutes. Drain and set aside. Drizzle a little peanut oil over the top.

Once all the dumplings have been poached, whisk sesame oil and peanut butter into boiling stock. Add hot pepper sauce, to taste. Adjust seasoning if necessary. Set aside.

In non-stick skillet, heat a little peanut oil. Grill dumplings, a few at a time.

Serve as appetizer with satay sauce.

WHAT TO DRINK?
This hors d'oeuvre is excellent with a Pinot Blanc or Alsatian Pinot Gris.

Once poached, the dumplings can be frozen. You may also freeze the sauce. To serve, just grill the thawed dumplings in a skillet and heat the satay sauce.

One word describes this dish: decadent! It's the perfect appetizer for a dinner with friends or an after-ski party. With a glass of red wine, some pieces of bread, the hot melted cheese, and a fire going in the fireplace, we're ready to solve the world's problems.

Melted Brie
with cranberries

PREPARATION TIME
10 MINUTES

WAITING TIME
20 MINUTES

COOKING TIME
20 MINUTES

SERVES
6

⅓ cup (75 mL) port wine
⅓ cup (75 mL) dried cranberries
1 red onion, finely chopped
2 Tbsp (25 mL) butter
¼ cup (50 mL) roasted pine nuts
¼ cup (50 mL) black olives, chopped
¾ lb (375 g) brie or Camembert
1 Tbsp (15 mL) fresh parsley, minced

Place rack in centre of oven. Preheat to 350°F (180°C).

In small bowl, pour port wine over cranberries. Let stand for 20 minutes.

In skillet, brown onion in butter for about 10 minutes. Deglaze the onions with cranberry and port mixture. Add pine nuts and olives.

Place cheese on a piece of 12-inch (30-cm) square aluminum foil. Bring foil up around cheese to prevent it from caving in while cooking. Spread onion-cranberry mixture on cheese, and place on cookie sheet.

Bake in oven for about 10 minutes. Remove and decorate with fresh parsley. Serve hot and whole in centre of table, with country bread or rusks.

WHAT TO DRINK?
A red wine
such as
St-Joseph or
Crozes-Hermitage

Everyone at our house loves cream of celery soup. I serve it garnished with walnuts and crumbled blue cheese. If you'd like to discover the unique taste of this cheese, here's a simple way.

Cream of Celery Soup
with walnuts and blue cheese

PREPARATION TIME
20 MINUTES

COOKING TIME
25 MINUTES

SERVES
4 TO 6

1 leek, white part only, chopped
2 Tbsp (25 mL) olive oil
10 celery stalks, cut into pieces
1 apple, peeled, cored and
    cut into pieces
¼ cup (50 mL) white wine or
    chicken stock
4 cups (1 L) chicken stock
¼ cup (50 mL) long grain rice
1 cup (250 mL) spinach, trimmed
½ cup (125 mL) sour cream or
    15% cooking cream
salt and pepper
¼ cup (50 mL) walnuts, finely chopped
¼ cup (50 mL) blue cheese,
    crumbled (optional)

In a medium saucepan, brown leek in oil over medium heat for about 2 minutes.

Add celery and apple. Deglaze with wine and reduce for 1 minute. Add stock and rice.

Cook uncovered over medium heat for about 15 minutes. Add spinach and continue cooking for 5 minutes.

Transfer to blender. Process. Return soup to saucepan and add cream. Stir and reheat without boiling.

Season with salt and pepper.

To serve, garnish with walnuts and cheese.

Clams
with white wine, tomatoes and fennel

PREPARATION TIME
15 MINUTES

WAITING TIME
2 HOURS

COOKING TIME
10 MINUTES

SERVES
4

32 small clams in shell
3 slices bacon, finely chopped
1 Tbsp (15 mL) butter
2 shallots, finely chopped
1 garlic clove, finely chopped
1 fennel bulb, cut into thin slices
3 plum tomatoes, peeled, seeded
   and diced
¼ cup (50 mL) white wine
½ cup (125 mL) chicken stock
1 Tbsp (15 mL) lemon juice
2 Tbsp (25 mL) fresh flat
   parsley, minced
1 green onion, chopped
pepper

Place clams in cold water. Let them soak for 2 hours, changing water 2 or 3 times. Rinse, drain and keep cold.

In a large skillet, brown bacon until golden. Add butter, shallots, garlic and fennel. Continue cooking for 3 minutes.

Add tomatoes, wine, stock, lemon juice and clams still in shell. Cover and cook over high heat for about 5 minutes or until clams open up. Sprinkle with parsley and green onion. Season with pepper and serve.

Clams often contain sand, which is why you need to soak them for about 2 hours before cooking them. Change the water 2 or 3 times while they're soaking. Don't leave them in water any longer, or they could die and become inedible. If clams aren't available, substitute mussels.

WHAT TO DRINK?
The fruity freshness of a Picpoul de Pinet will add to the pleasure of this beautiful appetizer.

Foie gras is a luxury item, so I prepare this recipe during the holiday season and invite friends who will appreciate its delicacy.

Foie Gras Terrine

PREPARATION TIME
15 MINUTES

WAITING TIME
36 HOURS

COOKING TIME
1 HOUR, 20 MINUTES

SERVES
8

Terrine

*1 raw whole duck liver (foie gras)
    of 1¼ lb / 625g*
½ tsp (2 mL) salt
freshly ground pepper
¼ cup (50 mL) white port wine

Jelly

1 envelope gelatin
1¼ cups (300 mL) Sauternes or ice cider

Terrine

Let foie gras stand at room temperature for 1 hour.

Cut foie gras down the middle, opening carefully. Remove large veins, using tweezers or tip of a paring knife. Place foie gras in dish. Season both sides with salt and pepper. Drizzle a little port wine over the top. Cover with plastic wrap and refrigerate for 12 hours.

Cut a piece of cardboard that's the same size as the loaf pan (terrine). Wrap cardboard with aluminum foil (to be used when terrine is refrigerated).

Remove foie gras from refrigerator and let stand for 30 minutes at room temperature.

Place rack in centre of oven. Preheat to 200°F (100°C).

Place foie gras in a 6- × 3½-inch (15- × 9-cm) terrine and cover with aluminum foil. Place terrine in double boiler. Add enough hot water to fill double boiler halfway up the terrine. Cook in oven for about one hour and 20 minutes, or until a meat thermometer inserted through the foil in the centre of the terrine indicates 130°F (55°C).

Remove terrine from double boiler. Remove foil and gently tip terrine (foie gras is very fragile) so that fat drips into a small bowl. Set fat aside in refrigerator and use to cook hash browns, fry mushrooms or sear steak.

Place cardboard covered with aluminum foil onto the foie gras. Press and hold in place using two small tin cans. Refrigerate for 24 hours.

To remove fois gras from terrine, soak base of the pan in boiling water. Turn out fois gras onto a plate and slice. Foie gras will keep in the refrigerator for a few days, if well wrapped.

Serve with *pain brioche* (bread with a brioche-like consistency and taste), *fleur de sel* and Sauternes or ice cider jelly.

Jelly

Empty envelope of gelatin into ¼ cup (50 mL) cold Sauternes or ice cider and let set for 2 minutes. In small saucepan, heat remaining wine. Add gelatin to the saucepan, stirring until melted. Pour the gelatin mixture into 8-inch (20-cm) square pan. Let set in refrigerator for about 2 hours. With the gelatin in the pan, cut into small cubes using a sharp knife. Lift cubes with spatula and place around foie gras slices.

WHAT TO DRINK?
It's traditional to serve Sauternes with foie gras; an Alsatian Pinot Gris is a great alternative.

Fig Crostini
with gorgonzola cheese

PREPARATION TIME
15 MINUTES

COOKING TIME
10 MINUTES

SERVES
8

8 green onions, finely chopped
2 garlic cloves, chopped
2 Tbsp (25 mL) olive oil
2 Tbsp (25 mL) balsamic vinegar
1 French baguette
4 large fresh figs, sliced
3 Tbsp (45 mL) walnuts, chopped
5 oz (150 g) Gorgonzola cheese,
*   cut into small pieces*
olive oil
pepper

Place rack on upper shelf of oven. Preheat to broil.

In a small skillet, soften green onions and garlic in olive oil. Add balsamic vinegar and reduce. Set aside.

Slice baguette horizontally. Remove both ends and cut eight 4-inch (10-cm) long pieces.

Spread onion mix on bread, then the figs. Sprinkle with walnuts, then cheese.

Drizzle a little olive oil over the crostini. Grill in oven for a few minutes. Season with pepper. Serve hot as hors d'oeuvre or appetizer.

If fresh figs aren't available, substitute fresh pear slices.

WHAT TO DRINK?
A dark beer,
rich and
smooth.

I love the crisp and slightly foggy fall mornings when we can still enjoy our coffee on the patio. Mushroom season is almost over, but delicious stocks, stews and steaming pies are just around the corner. The morning fog signals a new day, and I know that pleasure and cravings will transform my kitchen into a hangout for gluttons. Autumn is the best of both worlds. The earth is still warm with summer heat; in the sun, pistachio ice cream is still a scrumptious treat. But, when the sun goes down, we warm up with onion soup. But not just any onion soup! One with red onions, beer from a local brewery and cheddar cheese.

Onion Soup
with beer and cheddar cheese

¼ cup (50 mL) butter
8 red onions, sliced
2 garlic cloves, finely chopped
1 bottle locally brewed beer
    (341 mL), pale ale or other
3 cups (750 mL) beef stock
1 sprig of fresh thyme or ½ tsp
    (2 mL) dried thyme
1 bay leaf
1 juniper berry, crushed (optional)
1 Tbsp (15 mL) tomato paste
4 slices of bread, toasted, cut
    to same size as bowls
1 cup (250 mL) aged cheddar
    cheese, grated
salt and pepper

Place rack on oven's top shelf. Preheat to broil.

In a saucepan, melt butter. Add onions and soften over medium heat for 10 to 15 minutes, until they start to caramelize. Add garlic and continue cooking for 1 minute.

Add beer, stock, thyme, bay leaf, juniper berry and tomato paste. Stir well. Bring to a boil, cover and simmer for 15 minutes. Season to taste. Remove bay leaf.

Ladle soup into ovenproof bowls. Cover soup with slice of toasted bread sprinkled with cheese. Brown in oven and serve.

side by
side

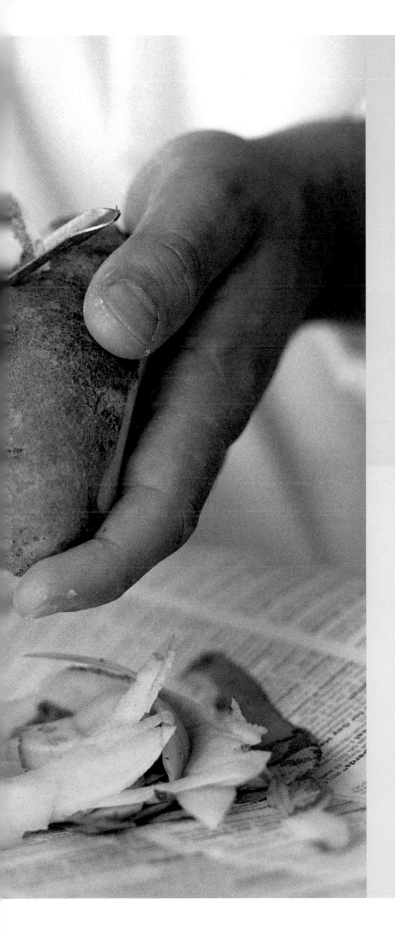

Salads and Vegetable Side Dishes

One summer, to my children's delight, my in-laws stayed with us while some repairs were being done to their house. My father-in-law had but one comment when he left: "They never eat potatoes in this family!" This isn't true. Sometimes, we eat blue potatoes! He was right about one thing: rice, pasta and couscous have become an important part of our meals. My childhood days, when potatoes were always on the menu, are long gone. Jules, these recipes are for you.

Potatoes
with cheddar cheese

PREPARATION TIME
15 MINUTES

COOKING TIME
50 MINUTES

SERVES
8

8 potatoes
⅓ cup (75 mL) olive oil
¼ cup (50 mL) fresh chives, minced
1 cup (250 mL) aged cheddar, grated
¼ cup (50 mL) bread crumbs
salt and pink pepper

Place rack in centre of oven. Preheat oven to 375°F (190°C).

Peel potatoes and cut them in half, lengthwise. Place halves flat on work surface. Slice them, but not completely (see photo on page 63).

In bowl, mix potatoes, olive oil and chives, making sure the oil gets between each slice. Season with salt and pepper.

Place potatoes on cookie sheet and bake in oven for about 35 minutes, basting potatoes a few times with remaining olive oil during cooking. Remove the potatoes from oven. Sprinkle with cheese and bread crumbs. Return potatoes to oven and cook until cheese has browned, about 15 minutes.

Gratin Dauphinois
scalloped potatoes

PREPARATION TIME
20 MINUTES

COOKING TIME
1 HOUR, 15 MINUTES

SERVES
6

2½ lb (1.2 kg) potatoes,
    peeled (about 6 large)
2 cups (500 mL) Emmenthal
    cheese, grated
1 cup (250 mL) 35% whipping cream
salt and pepper

Place rack in centre of oven. Preheat to 350°F (180°C).

Wash potatoes, pat dry and slice thinly with a mandoline. Don't rinse potato slices so as to retain as much starch as possible.

Butter sides and bottom of 12- × 8-inch (30- × 20-cm) pan. Cover bottom with potato slices.

Add a layer of cheese and cream. Season with salt and pepper. Alternating layers, continue in same manner, until all ingredients have been used. Cover with aluminum foil.

Cook in oven for 1 hour. Remove foil and continue cooking for about 15 minutes, until the top is golden. Let stand for 10 minutes and then cut into squares.

I love buttered asparagus—even more with this hollandaise sauce. I refrigerate the leftover sauce and serve it, cold and firm, on grilled fish the next day. Mmm!

Grilled Asparagus
and hollandaise sauce with tarragon

PREPARATION TIME
15 MINUTES

COOKING TIME
15 MINUTES

SERVES
6

36 asparagus spears, trimmed
olive oil
salt and pepper
½ cup (125 mL) 35% whipping cream,
    whipped
2 Tbsp (25 mL) fresh tarragon,
    minced

Hollandaise Sauce

3 Tbsp (40 mL) lemon juice
3 egg yolks
¾ cup (175 mL) butter cubes,
    at room temperature
salt and pepper

Asparagus

Place rack on upper shelf of oven. Preheat oven to Broil. Place asparagus on cookie sheet. Drizzle a little olive oil over the top. Season with salt and pepper. Broil in oven until *al dente*. Shake cookie sheet once while cooking.

Hollandaise Sauce

In upper part of double boiler, before heating, beat lemon juice with egg yolks. Place over simmering water and stir until mixture is hot.

Beat in the pieces of butter, one at a time. Each butter cube should be completely melted before adding the next one. Sauce shouldn't boil.

Remove the sauce from heat. Cool. Season with salt and pepper. Fold in whipped cream and fresh tarragon.

Top grilled asparagus with the hollandaise sauce. Serve as an appetizer or vegetable side dish.

WHAT TO DRINK?
An Alsatian
dry Muscat
for this
first course.

65

My wife, Brigitte, turned me on to quinoa. It looks like cereal and resembles couscous or bulgur. Botanically speaking, it's another story: quinoa is the fruit of a plant from the same family as beets and spinach. Once cooked, the small yellowish grains pop in your mouth, like caviar. You can find quinoa at natural food stores and more and more supermarkets.

Quinoa Salad
with beans

1 cup (250 mL) quinoa
7 oz (200 g) thin green beans, trimmed
1 can (19 oz/540 mL) kidney
*   beans, rinsed and drained*
2 green onions, finely chopped
½ English cucumber, peeled and diced
¼ cup (50 mL) olive oil
3 Tbsp (40 mL) white wine vinegar
1 Tbsp (15 mL) fresh tarragon, minced
a few drops of Tabasco sauce
salt and pepper

In a saucepan, cook quinoa in a large quantity of boiling salted water for about 15 minutes, or until the grains are tender but still crunchy. Rinse in cold water and drain well. Set aside.

Cook green beans in boiling salted water. Rinse in very cold water, drain and set aside.

Mix all ingredients in a salad bowl. Season with salt and pepper.

For best results, refrigerate salad for 1 hour before serving with grilled meat or fish.

I really enjoy the taste of olive oil and would use it in all my salads if I could! However, its flavour is too pronounced for certain salad dressings, like Caesar. If you want to use olive oil, mix half and half with vegetable oil (canola, corn or soybean).

Caesar Salad

PREPARATION TIME
25 MINUTES

COOKING TIME
15 MINUTES

SERVES
4

6 slices of bread, crust
    removed, cubed
¼ cup (50 mL) butter
10 slices bacon
1 large head of romaine
    lettuce, shredded

Dressing
1 egg yolk
1 Tbsp (15 mL) lemon juice
1 garlic clove, finely chopped
¾ cup (175 mL) vegetable oil
2 Tbsp (25 mL) capers, chopped
1 tsp (5 mL) anchovy paste
    (or 2 anchovies mashed
    with a wooden spoon)
¾ cup (175 mL) Parmigiano
    Reggiano cheese, grated

In skillet, brown bread cubes in butter for about 10 minutes. Set aside.

In same skillet, cook bacon until crispy. Drain using paper towels. Chop and set aside.

Dressing
In bowl, beat egg yolk, lemon juice and garlic. Add oil by pouring slowly while beating constantly until mixture thickens. Add capers, anchovy paste and a quarter of the cheese.

In salad bowl, mix lettuce, dressing, croutons and bacon. Sprinkle with remaining cheese; season with pepper. Serve immediately.

Potato Salad
with Jerusalem artichokes

PREPARATION TIME
15 MINUTES

COOKING TIME
30 MINUTES

SERVES
4 TO 6

1¼ lb (625 g) grelot *(very small)*
  potatoes
10 oz (300 g) Jerusalem
  artichokes, peeled
1 cup (250 mL) cucumber,
  peeled, seeded and diced
⅓ cup (75 mL) roasted walnut pieces
salt and pepper

Dressing
¾ cup (180 mL) mayonnaise
2 tsp (10 mL) white wine vinegar
zest and juice of 1 orange
2 Tbsp (25 mL) fresh chives, minced
1 tsp (5 mL) fresh thyme, leaves only
salt and pepper

Cook potatoes and artichokes, separately, in boiling salted water until tender, from 20 to 30 minutes. Drain and cool. Cut potatoes into quarters and artichokes into pieces of the same size.

Meanwhile, prepare dressing. In bowl, beat mayonnaise, vinegar, zest, orange juice, chives and thyme. Season with salt and pepper. Set aside.

Pour dressing into a large bowl. Add potatoes and artichokes, then cucumber and walnuts. Mix delicately. Season to taste. Serve immediately as a side dish with meat and poultry.

Some forgotten vegetables are making a comeback. That's the case with the Jerusalem artichoke, a tuber native to North America. It's called an artichoke because of its taste, which is similar to the more common one. It's available in the fall and can be refrigerated, for up to 4 months, in a plastic perforated bag. It can be cooked in a gratin, like potatoes, or in a soup. It will quickly darken when exposed to air so have a bowl of water, to which a drop of lemon juice has been added, ready when peeling this odd-shaped tuber.

My Salad Dressings

Parmesan and Black Olives

½ cup (125 mL) olive oil
2 Tbsp (25 mL) white wine vinegar
3 Tbsp (40 mL) grated Parmigiano Reggiano cheese
3 Tbsp (40 mL) black olives in oil,
    pitted and finely chopped
1 small garlic clove, finely chopped
1 Tbsp (15 mL) fresh flat parsley, minced
salt and pepper

Beat all ingredients in a bowl. This is a perfect dressing with a romaine lettuce salad.

Asian

½ cup (125 mL) vegetable oil
2 tsp (10 mL) toasted sesame oil
1 small garlic clove, finely chopped
1 Tbsp (15 mL) fresh ginger, finely chopped
3 Tbsp (40 mL) rice vinegar
½ tsp (2 mL) honey
salt and pepper

Beat all ingredients in a bowl. This dressing is delicious with a salad of bean sprouts, matchstick sweet peppers and green onion.

Blue Cheese

⅓ cup (75 mL) blue cheese
1 cup (250 mL) sour cream
1 Tbsp (15 mL) fresh flat parsley, minced
2 tsp (10 mL) lemon juice
pepper

Beat all ingredients in a small blender or food processor. This dressing enhances the flavour of spinach.

French

½ cup (125 mL) olive oil
2 Tbsp (25 mL) Dijon mustard
2 Tbsp (25 mL) white wine vinegar
1 tsp (5 mL) dried tarragon
salt and pepper

Beat all ingredients in a bowl. Serve with mesclun.

Beef Salad
with bean sprouts and green apples

PREPARATION TIME
20 MINUTES

COOKING TIME
10 MINUTES

SERVES
4 TO 6

butter, as needed
1 slice (1 lb / 454 g) cross
*   rib roast, boned*
3 green apples
3 cups (750 mL) bean sprouts
3 green onions, finely chopped
¼ cup (50 mL) fresh coriander, minced
½ cup (125 mL) roasted
*   peanuts, crushed*
salt and pepper

Dressing

2 Tbsp (30 mL) fresh lime juice
1 tsp (5 mL) sugar
1 Tbsp (15 mL) fish sauce
1 Tbsp (15 mL) non-toasted sesame oil
1 Tbsp (15 mL) soy sauce
1 small garlic clove, finely chopped
Pinch of cayenne pepper

In grooved skillet with some butter, or on barbecue, sear beef on both sides for about 5 minutes, until meat is cooked rare. Season with salt and pepper. Let stand for 5 minutes. Slice in thin strips and set aside.

Using a mandoline or well-sharpened knife, slice apples into thin matchsticks.

In bowl, mix beef, apples and other ingredients for salad.

Dressing

In bowl, beat ingredients and pour onto salad. Mix well and season to taste.

WHAT TO DRINK?
A chilled rosé
from Provence
goes perfectly
with this salad.

Root vegetables, other than carrots and potatoes, are seldom used in cooking. They're used mostly in stewed dishes. Yet they're filled with flavour and add to the look of a dish. Black salsify (also known as oyster plant), for example, looks like a long carrot with black skin and cream-coloured flesh that darkens quickly. To avoid blackening, dip salsify into water to which a drop of lemon juice has been added as soon as it's sliced. When I want to serve salsify during the weekend, I order them from my grocer a few days in advance.

Overlooked Root Vegetables
in glaze

PREPARATION TIME
10 MINUTES

COOKING TIME
50 MINUTES

SERVES
4

3 Tbsp (40 mL) butter
2 Tbsp (25 mL) honey
4 long thin carrots, peeled and
*   cut into 4 pieces, lengthwise*
4 small parsnips, peeled and cut into
*   4 pieces, lengthwise*
4 black salsify (optional), peeled and
*   cut into 2 or 3 pieces, lengthwise*
2 medium rapini, peeled and
*   cut into 6 pieces*
1 leek, white part only, cut into 1-inch
*   (2.5-cm) pieces*
1 onion, cut into pieces, or 12
*   small pickling onions*
2 tsp (10 mL) fresh thyme, leaves only
salt and pepper

Place rack in centre of oven. Preheat oven to 350°F (180°C).

In large ovenproof skillet, heat butter and honey. Add vegetables and thyme. Cook for about 10 minutes, over medium-high heat, without stirring too much, allowing vegetables to caramelize. Season with salt and pepper. Place skillet in oven and continue cooking for 40 minutes, or until vegetables are tender.

Delicious with beef, game meat, pork and poultry.

As a teenager, except for my mother's marinated beets, even Chinese water torture wouldn't have convinced me to eat this boring vegetable. To me, it seemed too sweet to be a vegetable, was forever staining everything and always came bland and boiled. I couldn't foresee a future for it. When the sugar refinery closed its doors in Saint-Hilaire, I thought that the beet's fate was finally sealed (even if it wasn't the same variety). Fortunately, tastes evolve. How did I manage to do without such a culinary pleasure for so long? It's true that a boiled beet remains uninspiring. But with butter, chives, fennel and sea salt or, better yet, in a salad with endives, pink grapefruit segments and olive oil, then we're talking!

Beets with Fennel

PREPARATION TIME
10 MINUTES

COOKING TIME
1 HOUR, 15 MINUTES

SERVES
6

*8 beets, peeled and cut
  into small pieces*
2 Tbsp (25 mL) olive oil
1 Tbsp (15 mL) fennel seeds
1½ tsp (7 mL) celery salt
6 garlic cloves, peeled
salt and pepper
*1 Tbsp (15 mL) fresh tarragon,
  minced*

Place rack in centre of oven. Preheat oven to 350°F (180°C).

In casserole dish, place all ingredients except for tarragon. Season with salt and pepper.

Cook in oven for about 1 hour and 15 minutes, stirring from time to time.

Remove from oven, take out garlic cloves, mash them and mix them with the beets. Sprinkle with tarragon.

Serve hot with meat or poultry.

In addition to the common deep red, we now find beets that are white, golden yellow and even two-toned (red and white). Are they interesting to cook? It depends. Cooked the same amount of time, red beets are firmer to the bite and less sweet than the yellow ones. For me, the latter taste much better. They also keep their beautiful colour when cooked, which isn't the case with the two-toned ones. To keep the gorgeous appearance of the two-tones, serve them raw, in salads.

Maple-Glazed Bok Choy

PREPARATION TIME
5 MINUTES

COOKING TIME
8 MINUTES

SERVES
4

*1 large bok choy, or 4 small ones,
   6 oz (175 g) each
1 Tbsp (15 mL) non-toasted sesame oil
1 garlic clove, chopped
salt and pepper
2 Tbsp (25 mL) soy sauce
¼ cup (50 mL) maple syrup
2 green onions, chopped*

Cut bok choy into 1-inch (2.5-cm) slices, diagonally.

In wok or large skillet, heat oil. Stir-fry bok choy with garlic for about 5 minutes, over medium heat. Season with salt and pepper.

Add soy sauce, maple syrup and green onions. Continue cooking over high heat for about 3 minutes. Season to taste.

Serve with grilled pork tenderloin or poultry, such as Tea-Smoked Chicken (recipe on page 129).

Toasted sesame oil has more flavour than non-toasted. Read your recipe carefully before using one or the other. If you don't have non-toasted sesame oil, you can replace it by one-third toasted sesame oil and two-thirds peanut or canola oil. To get 1 Tbsp (15 mL) non-toasted sesame oil, use 1 tsp (5 mL) toasted sesame oil mixed with 2 tsp (10 mL) peanut or canola oil.

My Mashed Vegetables

Mashed Celeriac with Spinach

PREPARATION TIME **30 MINUTES**
COOKING TIME **15 MINUTES**
SERVES **6**

8 cups (2 L) celeriac (about
    4 at 1 lb / 500 g each),
    peeled and cubed
2 Tbsp (25 mL) olive oil
6 cups (1.5 L) fresh
    spinach, trimmed
¼ cup (50 mL) butter
salt and pepper

Place celeriac in saucepan and
cover with lightly salted cold
water. Bring to a boil and cook
until tender. Drain. Return to
heat and continue cooking for
a few seconds until water has
evaporated completely. Set aside.

In saucepan, heat oil. Add spinach
and cook until wilted. Strain
through a colander, pressing firmly.

In food processor, blend
vegetables with butter. Season
with salt and pepper.

Serve with duck or chicken.

Mashed Root Vegetables

PREPARATION TIME **15 MINUTES**
COOKING TIME **35 MINUTES**
SERVES **6**

4 cups (1 L) potatoes (about 4
    or 1½ lb / 750 g), peeled
    and cut into large cubes
2 cups (500 mL) turnips (about
    ½ medium-sized), peeled
    and cut into small cubes
¼ cup (50 mL) 15% cream,
    approximately
¼ cup (50 mL) butter
salt and pepper
3 Tbsp (40 mL) fresh flat
    parsley, minced
2 sprigs thyme, leaves only

Place vegetables in saucepan and
cover with lightly salted cold water.
Bring to a boil and cook until tender.
Drain. Return to heat and continue
cooking for a few seconds until
water has evaporated completely.

Using a pestle, mash vegetables.
Add cream and butter. Beat
with electric mixer until well
mixed. Season with salt,
pepper, parsley and thyme.

Delicious with beef or veal.

Mashed Potatoes with Candied Garlic

PREPARATION TIME **30 MINUTES**
COOKING TIME **1 HOUR, 20 MINUTES**
SERVES **6**

1 garlic bulb
7 cups (1.75 L) potatoes
    (about 8 medium-sized),
    peeled and cut into pieces
½ cup (125 mL) olive oil
salt and pepper

Place rack in centre of oven.
Preheat to 350°F (180°C).

Slice top of garlic bulb. Wrap in
aluminum foil and cook in oven
for about 45 minutes. Cool.

Place potatoes in saucepan and cover
with lightly salted cold water. Bring
to a boil and cook until tender.
Drain, reserving some of the liquid.
Return potatoes to heat and continue
cooking for a few seconds until
water has evaporated completely.

With pestle, mash potatoes coarsely.
Squeeze garlic head over potatoes
so that garlic flesh falls into them.
Add oil and beat with electric mixer.
If needed, add reserved cooking
liquid for a creamier texture.
Season with salt and pepper.

Perfect side dish for meat,
poultry and fish.

dolce vita

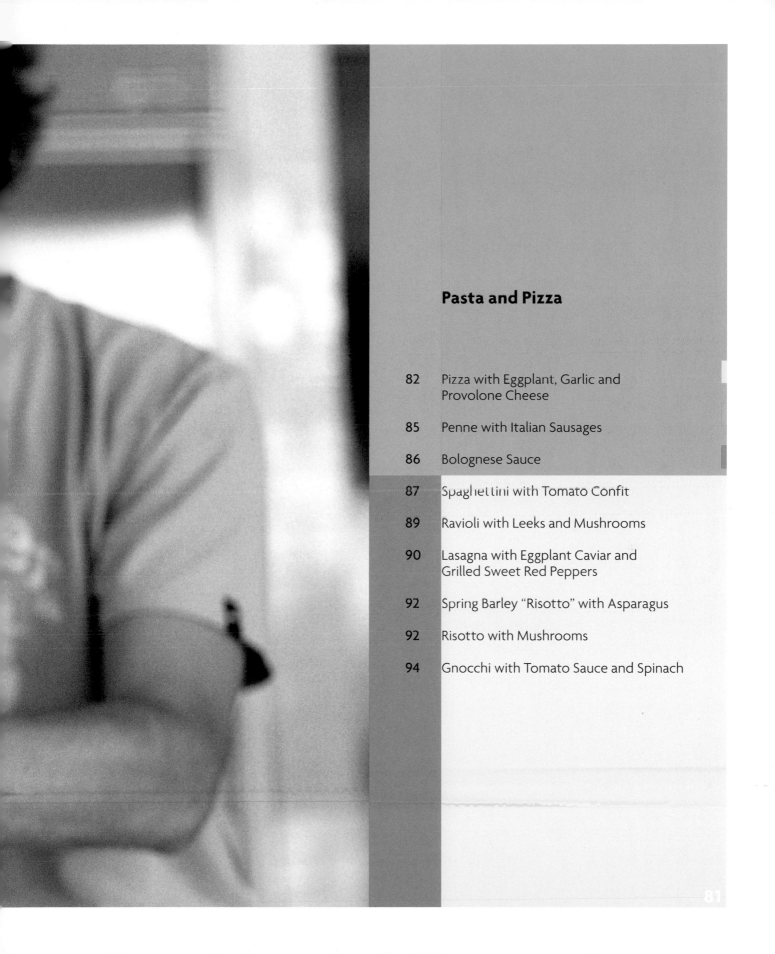

Pasta and Pizza

Pizza with Eggplant
garlic and provolone cheese

PREPARATION TIME
40 MINUTES

WAITING TIME
35 MINUTES

COOKING TIME
1 HOUR, 20 MINUTES

MAKES
TWO 8-INCH (20-CM)

PIZZAS

Homemade Pizza Dough

1 cup (250 mL) warm water
1 tsp (5 mL) fast-rising yeast
1 tsp (5 mL) sugar
2 cups (500 mL) flour
1 tsp (5 mL) salt

Pizza Sauce

3 garlic cloves, chopped
2 Tbsp (25 mL) olive oil
1 can (28 oz / 796 mL) plum tomatoes
1 Tbsp (15 mL) dried basil
1 Tbsp (15 mL) dried oregano
salt and pepper

Garnish

2 garlic bulbs
8 to 10 thin slices of medium-
    sized eggplant
olive oil
salt
cornmeal
½ cup (125 mL) pizza sauce
8 slices provolone cheese
fresh basil, minced

Homemade Pizza Dough

In bowl, mix water, yeast and sugar. Let stand for about 5 minutes, until foam appears on top of mixture.

In food processor, working with the plastic blade or dough hook, mix flour and salt. Process on medium speed and add yeast mixture until soft ball forms.

Remove dough from bowl and knead for a few minutes, while sprinkling with flour to prevent dough from sticking. Place dough in a lightly oiled bowl and cover with clean cloth. Let dough rise for about 30 minutes in a lukewarm place. Afterwards, cut it in half.

Pizza Sauce

In saucepan, brown chopped garlic in oil. Crush tomatoes with your hands and add to saucepan with remaining ingredients. Slowly simmer for about 20 minutes, without covering. This recipe yields 3 cups (750 mL). You may freeze leftover sauce.

Garnish

Place rack on bottom level of oven. Preheat to 400°F (200°C).

Chop the tops off the garlic bulbs. Place the bulbs on aluminum foil and wrap well. Cook in oven for about 45 minutes. Set aside.

Preheat pizza stone in oven.

In skillet, brown eggplant in olive oil (be generous with the oil so that the eggplant browns well). Season with salt and set aside.

Sprinkle some cornmeal on pizza board. Roll dough to obtain two 8-inch (20-cm) crusts. Slide the first one on the board.

Press out the roasted garlic cloves from the bulbs to extract as much as possible of the cooked garlic and spread half on the first pizza crust. Add and spread some sauce. Sprinkle with eggplant and cheese. Slide pizza on pizza stone. Cook in oven for about 15 minutes. Meanwhile, prepare the second pizza. Garnish with fresh basil and serve.

WHAT TO DRINK?

Stay regional
with an Italian red:
a light Chianti
Classico.

Penne with Italian Sausages

PREPARATION TIME
25 MINUTES

COOKING TIME
25 MINUTES

SERVES
4

12 plum tomatoes
4 hot Italian sausages
1 onion, finely chopped
4 garlic cloves, finely chopped
⅓ cup (75 mL) olive oil
½ cup (125 mL) red wine
1 Tbsp (15 mL) fresh oregano,
    leaves only
¼ cup (50 mL) fresh basil, minced
4 cups (1 L) penne with ridges,
    cooked and hot
salt and pepper

Using a sharp knife, make an incision in the form of an X on the end of each tomato, opposite from stem. In boiling water, blanch tomatoes for 1 to 2 minutes, depending on how ripe they are (the riper they are, the faster they'll blanch). Afterwards, plunge the tomatoes into cold water. Peel, cut in half and seed them.

Prick sausages with fork and boil them for 5 minutes. Cool and cut into medium-sized slices. Set aside.

In saucepan, cook onion and garlic in olive oil. Add sausages and continue cooking until onion starts to brown. Add wine and reduce by half.

Add tomatoes, reduce heat and simmer for about 15 minutes, stirring occasionally. Add oregano and basil. Fold in cooked pasta and mix well. Season with salt and pepper. Serve immediately.

WHAT TO DRINK?
A good Italian
red such as
Montepulciano
d'Abruzzo.

I remember the aroma of the spaghetti sauce painstakingly prepared by my father every Saturday afternoon. Our clothes would smell of caramelized onions, garlic and simmering tomatoes. After pasta, it was naptime. Quiet bliss. We all have within us profound memories of smells and tastes that give us a sense of calm and security. To ground oneself, some people need hypnotherapy, regression to the womb, or St. John's wort. But for most of us, the act of putting a piece of food full of memories in our mouth is as good as any shaman. Some dishes are comfort foods, good for your soul.

Bolognese Sauce

PREPARATION TIME
20 MINUTES

COOKING TIME
2 HOURS, 30 MINUTES

SERVES
6 TO 8

2 oz (50 g) mild pancetta (Italian bacon), thinly sliced
¼ cup (50 mL) olive oil
2 onions, finely chopped
2 carrots, diced
2 celery stalks, diced
6 garlic cloves, finely chopped
2 lb (1 kg) lean ground beef
1½ cups (375 mL) red wine
1 cup (250 mL) milk
2 cans (28 oz / 796 mL each) plum tomatoes
1 Tbsp (15 mL) dried oregano
2 Tbsp (25 mL) dried basil
2 bay leaves
nutmeg, to taste
pepper flakes, to taste
salt and pepper

In a medium saucepan, brown pancetta in olive oil. Add vegetables and garlic. Cook for a few minutes. Add meat and break it up over high heat until cooking juices have evaporated.

Add wine and reduce by half. Add milk and simmer gently for 5 minutes.

Add remaining ingredients and continue cooking over low heat for about 2 hours, without covering.

WHAT TO DRINK?
A Sangiovese
di Romagna.

This recipe is a winner every time. Everyone loves pasta. This one is different due to the tomato confit. For those pressed for time, making tomato confit is a good compromise to drying tomatoes in the oven. This technique requires about 2 hours and 30 minutes cooking time, but there's no need to watch over the pot, and it takes only 10 minutes to prepare. Once the confit tomatoes are ready, I use them immediately or freeze them, 10 to a freezer bag, on which I write the date. Remember that the longer the tomatoes stay in the oven, the less water they'll retain. It's best to taste a piece of tomato after two hours of cooking to determine how you like them. Afterwards, you'll be able to cook them with your eyes closed.

Spaghettini
with tomato confit

PREPARATION TIME
25 MINUTES

COOKING TIME
2 HOURS, 45 MINUTES

SERVES
4

Tomato Confit

1½ lb (750 g) plum tomatoes,
    about 10
3 Tbsp (45 mL) olive oil
2 tsp (10 mL) dried basil
1 tsp (5 mL) dried oregano
sea salt and freshly ground pepper

Pasta and Sauce

½ cup (125 mL) olive oil
crushed pepper flakes, to taste
2 red onions, minced
2 garlic cloves, finely chopped
½ lb (225 g) mushrooms, quartered
1 recipe of tomato confit,
    cut into little pieces
¼ cup (50 mL) white wine
¼ cup (50 mL) chicken stock
¾ lb (375 g) spaghettini, cooked
    and hot
½ cup (125 mL) fresh basil, minced
shavings of Parmigiano Reggiano
    or pecorino cheese

Tomato Confit

Place rack in centre of oven. Preheat to 200°F (100°C).

Wash tomatoes and cut in half. Remove tomato hearts and seeds.

In bowl, mix together all ingredients. Place tomatoes on cookie sheet, round side up.

Cook in oven for about 2 hours and 30 minutes, depending on the size of the tomatoes. (If cooked for 15 hours, you'll get dried tomatoes.)

Pasta and Sauce

In saucepan, heat oil and pepper flakes. Add onions and soften slightly. Add garlic and mushrooms. Continue cooking until mushrooms lose their water.

Add tomatoes and wine. Cook for 1 minute. Season with salt and pepper.

Add stock and pasta. Stir well to reheat. Season to taste. At the last minute, add basil.

Serve topped with cheese.

WHAT TO DRINK?
Opt for a
Dolcetta d'Alba.

The Tomato Confit recipe can be doubled or tripled. These tomatoes are delicious in a soup or as antipasti.

Ravioli with Leeks
and mushrooms

Stuffing

2 Tbsp (25 mL) butter
2½ cups (625 mL) leeks (about 2),
    white part only, finely minced
1 garlic clove, finely chopped
½ cup (125 mL) 35% cream
2 cups (500 mL) fresh spinach,
    trimmed and chopped
salt and pepper
¼ cup (50 mL) grated
    Parmigiano Reggiano
1 Tbsp (15 mL) flat parsley, minced
1 Tbsp (15 mL) fresh chives, minced

Ravioli

40 egg roll wrappers, thawed (about
    one 1 lb / 454 g package)
3 Tbsp (45 mL) olive oil

Garnish

3½ oz (100 g) hot pancetta,
    diced
3 Tbsp (45 mL) olive oil
2 shallots, chopped
2 garlic cloves, finely chopped
4 cups (1 L) shiitake or other
    mushrooms, stems removed, sliced
1 Tbsp (15 mL) flat parsley, minced
1 green onion, finely chopped
½ cup (125 mL) chicken stock
salt and pepper
¼ cup (50 mL) Parmigiano
    Reggiano, grated

Stuffing

In skillet, melt butter over medium-high heat. Add leeks and garlic, and brown slowly until tender. Add cream and simmer for about 5 minutes, until mixture thickens. Add spinach and cook until wilted. Season with salt and pepper. Transfer to bowl. Cool. Add Parmesan and herbs.

Ravioli

Place 4 wrappers on work surface. With a spoon, place 1 Tbsp (15 mL) of stuffing in centre of each wrapper. Brush wrappers with some water, and cover with second wrapper. Press wrappers all around stuffing to seal.

With a round cookie cutter (3 inch / 7.5 cm), cut each wrapper to form ravioli. Press sides again to seal. Repeat with remaining ingredients.

In a large saucepan of boiling, salted water, cook ravioli for about 5 minutes. Drain and place in bowl with olive oil.

Garnish

In large skillet, brown pancetta in oil.

Add shallots, garlic and mushrooms. Cook for 3 to 4 minutes. Add parsley, green onion and stock. Season to taste. Add ravioli and mix carefully. Sprinkle with Parmesan. Season with pepper. Serve immediately.

WHAT TO DRINK?
A good Merlot or
Cabernet Franc
from the Niagara
region will
complement this
dish beautifully.

Not so long ago, all lasagna were the same. Nowadays, layer still follows layer, but they're always different. Neither are they as thick as before, and they're more varied and subtle. In my recipe, everything is easy to prepare. Of course, you must take the time to cook the eggplants and grill the sweet peppers. Grilled peppers bought in jars, especially when out-of-season peppers are expensive, can replace the fresh ones.

Lasagna with Eggplant Caviar
and grilled sweet red peppers

PREPARATION TIME
20 MINUTES

COOKING TIME
1 HOUR, 30 MINUTES

SERVES
4 TO 6

3 sweet red peppers
2 eggplants
salt and pepper
4 cups (1 L) tomato sauce,
    homemade or store-bought
9 lasagna noodles, cooked
½ cup (125 mL) fresh basil, minced
6½ oz (200 g) mozzarella, sliced

Place rack in top of oven. Preheat oven to broil.

Cut peppers in half, seed and place on cookie sheet, skin side up. Grill peppers under broiler until skin darkens. Place peppers in an airtight container and cool. Remove skin and set aside.

Place rack in centre of oven and preheat to 350°F (180°C). Prick eggplants with a fork and place on a cookie sheet. Cook in oven for about 1 hour. Cool and cut in half, lengthwise. Using a spoon, remove flesh and mash in blender or with a potato masher. Season with salt and pepper. Set aside.

To make the lasagna, cover bottom of an 11- × 7-inch (28- × 18-cm) pan with half of the tomato sauce. Lay three pasta strips on top of the sauce. Cover with sweet peppers and basil. Place three other strips and cover with the eggplant caviar. Place last three strips on caviar and top with the remaining tomato sauce. Cover with cheese.

Cook in oven for about 20 minutes. Brown under broiler.

WHAT TO DRINK?
A red Italian from the Friuli region will make a tasty companion.

Spring Barley "Risotto"
with asparagus

PREPARATION TIME
20 MINUTES

COOKING TIME
50 MINUTES

SERVES
4

¾ cup (175 mL) pearl barley
1 onion, finely chopped
2 Tbsp (25 mL) olive oil
3 Tbsp (45 mL) butter
¼ cup (50 mL) white wine
3 cups (750 mL) chicken stock
1 cup (250 mL) fresh asparagus,
    cut in half, lengthwise, and
    then in ½ inch (1 cm) pieces
¾ cup (175 mL) freshly grated
    Parmigiano Reggiano
1 cup (250 mL) fresh basil, minced
salt and pepper

In saucepan, brown barley and onion in olive oil and 2 Tbsp (25 mL) of butter over medium heat until onion is translucent, about 5 minutes. Deglaze with white wine.

Add stock. Bring to boil, cover and simmer over low heat for about 30 minutes, stirring occasionally. Remove cover and stir continuously until liquid is almost completely absorbed, about 10 minutes. Add asparagus and cook for 5 minutes or until asparagus are *al dente*.

Fold in remaining butter, Parmesan and basil. Season to taste.

Delicious with meat, poultry and fish.

Risotto with Mushrooms

PREPARATION TIME
10 MINUTES

COOKING TIME
30 MINUTES

SERVES
4

4 cups (1 L) of a selection of
    mushrooms, coarsely
    chopped (¾ lb / 375 g)
¼ cup (50 mL) olive oil
½ cup (125 mL) shallots, chopped
¼ cup (50 mL) butter
1½ cups (375 mL) arborio rice
½ cup (125 mL) white wine
4 cups (1 L) chicken stock,
    hot or warm
¾ cup (175 mL) grated
    Parmigiano Reggiano
a few drops of truffle oil (optional)
sea salt and fresh ground pepper
shavings of Parmigiano Reggiano

In saucepan, fry mushrooms in olive oil. Season with salt and pepper. Set aside.

In same saucepan, brown shallots in butter. Add rice and cook for 1 minute over medium-high heat, stirring to coat well.

Deglaze with wine and cook over medium heat, stirring until liquid is almost completely absorbed. Add stock, about ¾ cup (175 mL) at a time, stirring often. Add stock when wooden spoon leaves a trail when passed through rice. After about 20 minutes, the rice should be *al dente*, having absorbed most of the liquid. It should have a creamy texture.

Add cheese and mushrooms. Season to taste. Add truffle oil, if desired.

Season with pepper and sprinkle with Parmesan. Serve immediately.

WHAT TO DRINK?
An Italian is a
must, such as
a Barbera d'Asti,
clean to the taste,
with a fine bouquet.

Gnocchi
with tomato sauce and spinach

PREPARATION TIME
45 MINUTES

WAITING TIME
1 HOUR, 30 MINUTES

COOKING TIME
50 MINUTES

SERVES
4 TO 6

Gnocchi

1 lb 7 oz (700 g) Idaho potatoes, whole
     and unpeeled (about 2 large ones)
1 egg
3 cups (750 mL) flour, approximately
2 tsp (10 mL) salt
½ cup (125 mL) grated Parmigiano
     Reggiano, approximately

Tomato Sauce and Spinach

6 plum tomatoes
1 shallot, chopped
1 Tbsp (15 mL) butter
1 tsp (5 mL) lemon juice
½ cup (125 mL) white wine
½ cup (125 mL) chicken stock
1 cup (250 mL) 35% whipping cream
½ cup (125 mL) grated
     Parmigiano Reggiano
3 cups (750 mL) fresh spinach,
     trimmed and chopped
1 Tbsp (15 mL) fresh basil, minced
1 Tbsp (15 mL) fresh oregano,
     leaves only
salt and pepper

Gnocchi

Place potatoes in saucepan and cover with cold water. Season with salt. Cook until tender. Drain. Cool and peel. Mash potatoes with a potato masher or pestle. Set aside in refrigerator for at least 1 hour.

Make a well in middle of cold potatoes. Break in egg and mix well. Add flour, salt and Parmesan. Mix.

On a work surface, knead potato dough until it becomes supple and smooth. Add flour as needed. Let stand for 30 minutes.

Divide into four parts. Form 4 rolls, ½ inch (1 cm) in diameter. Immediately cut each into ½-inch (1-cm) pieces. Sprinkle with flour. Roll each piece with the back of a fork to shape into small cylinders. Place finished gnocchi on floured cookie sheet.

In large saucepan with boiling salted water, cook gnocchi, a few at a time, 4 to 5 minutes or until they float to top of water. Drain and mix with hot tomato sauce. Sprinkle with more Parmesan.

Tomato Sauce and Spinach

Using a sharp knife, make X-shaped incision on the end of each tomato, opposite stem. In boiling water, blanch for 1 to 2 minutes, according to their degree of ripeness. Afterwards, place them in cold water and peel, seed and cut in half.

In saucepan, brown shallots in butter. Add tomatoes, lemon juice, wine and stock. Reduce by half. Add cream and reduce until thick. Add Parmesan, spinach, basil and oregano. Cook for 1 minute. Season with salt and pepper.

WHAT TO DRINK?
A good red wine
from Sicily,
such as Corvo.

You can make gnocchi ahead of time, cutting your cooking time in half. They'll keep in the refrigerator for 2 to 3 days and can also be frozen. To serve them, just cook them quickly in boiling salted water.

craving for
fish

"If I catch ya, I'll eat ya!"
MY DAUGHTER JEANNE, 16 MONTHS

Fish and Seafood

Shrimp
with garlic and pastis

2 fennel bulbs
3 Tbsp (45 mL) melted butter
5 garlic cloves
2 shallots, chopped
¼ cup (50 mL) olive oil
1 lb (500 g) raw shrimps,
    peeled and deveined
1 tsp (5 mL) fennel seeds
¼ cup (50 mL) pastis (licorice-
    flavoured liqueur)
¼ cup (50 mL) 35% whipping cream
salt and pepper

Cut fennel bulbs in half and remove cores.
Cut into thin slices diagonally. Cook by steaming
until *al dente*. Mix fennel with butter and season
with salt and pepper. Keep warm and set aside.

Cut garlic into thin slices. In saucepan, slowly cook garlic
and shallots in olive oil for 10 minutes. Increase heat.
Add shrimps and fennel. Stir for 1 minute and add pastis.

Cook for 2 minutes and add heavy cream. Reduce
for about 2 minutes. Season with salt and pepper.

Serve shrimps with fennel. Pasta coated with
olive oil and sea salt goes well with this dish.

WHAT TO DRINK?
A white wine from
the south of France,
either from Provence,
Côtes-du-Rhône or
Coteaux du Languedoc.

Crab Cakes
with cucumber sauce or salsa

Cucumber Sauce

1 cup (250 mL) plain yogurt
    (Mediterranean style)
½ cup (125 mL) peeled cucumber,
    seeded and diced
1 tsp (5 mL) paprika
a pinch of cayenne pepper
½ garlic clove, finely chopped
salt and pepper

Salsa

6 red tomatoes, seeded
2 green onions, chopped
1 garlic clove, finely chopped
3 Tbsp (45 mL) olive oil
2 Tbsp (25 mL) fresh coriander, minced
Tabasco sauce, to taste
salt and pepper

Crab Cakes

1 lb (500 g) crabmeat,
    thawed and well drained
¼ cup (50 mL) mayonnaise
3 green onions, finely chopped
2 garlic cloves, finely chopped
2 Tbsp (25 mL) Dijon mustard
1½ cups (375 mL) fresh bread crumbs
2 eggs
Tabasco sauce, to taste
1 Tbsp (15 mL) Worcestershire sauce
salt and pepper
¼ cup (50 mL) fine cornmeal
½ cup (125 mL) vegetable oil

Cucumber Sauce

In medium bowl, mix all ingredients. Refrigerate.
Serve cold.

Salsa

In food processor, pulse one half (three) of the
tomatoes. Dice the other half.

In bowl, mix diced and ground tomatoes with
remaining ingredients. Refrigerate. Serve cold.

Crab Cakes

In bowl, mix all ingredients except corn flour
and vegetable oil. Season with salt and pepper.
Shape into cakes 3 inches (7.5 cm) in diameter and
1 inch (2.5 cm) thick. Dip each cake into corn flour.

In non-stick skillet, heat half the oil. Add half of the
crab cakes and brown for about 6 minutes per side.
Brown remaining cakes, using additional oil as necessary.

Serve two crab cakes per person as a main dish,
one if serving as an appetizer. Serve with salsa
or cucumber sauce.

WHAT TO DRINK?
A good
well-chilled rosé.

Salmon Rosettes
with fennel and cream

PREPARATION TIME
25 MINUTES

COOKING TIME
20 MINUTES

SERVES
4

1 large fennel bulb
2 Tbsp (25 mL) butter
½ cup (125 mL) 15% cream
1 lb (500 g) salmon fillet
salt and pepper
black lumpfish eggs, to decorate
chives, to decorate

Place rack in centre of oven. Preheat to 425°F (220°C).

Set aside fennel leaves for decoration. Cut bulb in half, remove core and thinly slice fennel.

In saucepan, soften fennel in butter for about 2 minutes. Add cream. Season with salt and pepper.

Cover and simmer for 10 minutes, stirring from time to time. Cool

Slice salmon very thinly, as you would with smoked salmon. Place four 5-inch (12-cm) squares of parchment paper on a cookie sheet. Place a round cookie cutter 2 inches (5 cm) high and 3 inches (7.5 cm) in diameter on one of the squares.

Spread one quarter of cooked fennel into cookie cutter and press lightly with the back of spoon. Spread one quarter of the salmon on top of the fennel, so that it's completely covered. Form a flower or rosette with last slice of salmon by twisting it into a spiral. Season with salt and pepper. Carefully remove cookie cutter. Repeat steps.

Cook in oven about 10 minutes. Using a spatula, carefully place each rosette on a warm plate. Decorate with lumpfish eggs and chives.

WHAT TO DRINK?
A Côtes du Rhône
or a white
Costières du Nîmes.

If you don't have a cookie cutter for this recipe, use a tin can that's the same size, with both ends removed.

Skate with Hazelnut Butter
and capers

PREPARATION TIME
10 MINUTES

COOKING TIME
20 MINUTES

SERVES
4

6 cups (1.5 L) water
1 onion, quartered
1 carrot, cut into chunks
1 celery stalk, cut into chunks
1 sprig of thyme
1 bay leaf
¼ cup (50 mL) white wine vinegar
1 Tbsp (15 mL) coarse salt
2 ½ lb (1.2 kg) skate, skin removed, cut in four and rinsed

Hazelnut Butter with Capers
½ cup (125 mL) butter
2 Tbsp (25 mL) lemon juice
3 Tbsp (45 mL) capers
3 Tbsp (45 mL) fresh parsley, minced
salt and pepper

In large saucepan, bring water, vegetables, thyme, bay leaf, vinegar and coarse salt to a boil. Remove from heat and cool.

Place skate wings in saucepan. Bring to a boil, reduce heat and cook over low heat for about 7 minutes or until flesh flakes easily. Skim foam from surface while cooking.

Hazelnut Butter with Capers
Meanwhile, gently cook butter until browned and smelling of hazelnut. Be careful not to burn the butter. Remove from heat. Add lemon juice, capers and parsley. Season with salt and pepper. Pour onto the skate. Serve with grilled vegetables.

WHAT TO DRINK?
Treat yourself to
a great white wine
from Burgundy.

This hazelnut butter with capers is delicious served with grilled salmon, halibut or almost any type of fish.

Competition is strong. Pizza can be delivered within a half hour. The goal is, therefore, to cook a quick meal more delicious and cheaper than ordered pizza.

Mussels Marinière

PREPARATION TIME
10 MINUTES

COOKING TIME
10 MINUTES

SERVES
**4 AS AN APPETIZER OR
2 AS A MAIN COURSE**

4 shallots, chopped
⅓ cup (75 mL) butter, softened
1 cup (250 mL) celery or
    fennel bulb, minced
1½ cups (375 mL) white wine
1 bag of mussels (2 lb / 1 kg),
    trimmed and washed
3 Tbsp (45 mL) flour
salt and pepper

In large saucepan, slowly cook shallots in 2 Tbsp (25 mL) butter for about 2 minutes, without colouring. Add celery or fennel and continue cooking for 2 to 3 minutes. Pour in white wine and bring to boil.

As soon as it boils, add mussels and cover saucepan. Cook over high heat until shells open, about 5 minutes. Discard any unopened mussels.

Beat remaining butter and flour to make a smooth paste.

Remove mussels and place on warm serving plate, leaving stock in saucepan. Gradually whisk the butter paste into the stock. Season to taste.

Pour sauce over mussels and serve.

WHAT TO DRINK?
A Canadian
Pinot Blanc
from the
Okanagan Valley.

If mussels are open before cooking, just tap the open shell. If it closes up, the mussel is still alive. If the tapped shell doesn't close, throw it out; it's a sign that it's dead. After cooking, throw out any mussels that have remained closed.

Fish in Salt Crust

PREPARATION TIME
15 MINUTES

COOKING TIME
45 MINUTES

SERVES
2

8 cups (2 L) coarse salt
½ cup (125 mL) flour
6 egg whites
¼ cup (50 mL) water
3 sprigs fresh thyme
3 sprigs fresh dill
3 bay leaves
3 slices of lemon
1 whole fish (snapper, striped bass
    or other), 3 lb (1.5 kg)
    with scales intact*
lemon juice and olive oil

Place rack in centre of oven. Preheat to 450°F (230°C). Cover bottom of cookie sheet with parchment paper.

In small bowl, mix salt and flour. Add egg whites and water. Mix and set aside.

Using scissors, remove fish fins (or ask the fishmonger to do it for you).

Place thyme, dill, bay leaves and lemon slices inside fish.

Spread one third of salt mixture onto parchment paper, to cover length of fish. Place fish on salt bed and cover with remaining salt mix, pressing well, to form an even crust.

Bake fish in oven about 45 minutes.

Remove fish from the cookie sheet and place it on a cutting board. Using a mallet, break the crust to extract the fish. Remove the skin and lift out the fillets.

To serve, drizzle a little lemon juice and olive oil over the fish.

AS FOR WINE?
A sumptuous
Crozes-Hermitage
or a white
Hermitage.

*Make sure the fish isn't scaled when you buy it. A fish without scales will absorb too much salt and its skin will be difficult to remove.

Scallops Flavoured
with lemon and basil

PREPARATION TIME
30 MINUTES

COOKING TIME
20 MINUTES

SERVES
4

Lemon-Flavoured Cream

1 cup (250 mL) 35% cream
¼ cup (50 mL) chicken stock
zest of 1 lemon
1 tsp (5 mL) lemon juice
salt and pepper

Basil-Flavoured Oil

¼ cup (50 mL) olive oil
¼ cup (50 mL) fresh basil, minced
½ tsp (2 mL) lemon juice
salt and pepper

Julienne-Style Vegetables

⅓ cup (75 mL) butter
6 carrots, peeled and cut into matchsticks
1 leek, cut into matchsticks

Scallops

20 large scallops
2 Tbsp (25 mL) olive oil
salt and pepper

Lemon-Flavoured Cream

In saucepan, mix all ingredients. Cook over medium heat for about 15 minutes, until the liquid reduces by one half. Season with salt and pepper. Keep warm.

Basil-Flavoured Oil

Beat all ingredients using small hand-blender or whisk. Set aside.

Julienne Vegetables

In skillet, melt 3 Tbsp (45 mL) butter over medium heat. Add vegetables and cook for about 6 minutes. Season with salt and pepper. Keep warm.

Scallops

Place rack in centre of oven. Preheat to 375°F (190°C).

Pat scallops dry on paper towel.

In skillet, heat 1 Tbsp (15 mL) butter and 1 Tbsp (15 mL) olive oil over high heat. Grill half of the scallops for about 1 minute on each side. Season with salt and pepper. Set aside on a cookie sheet. Repeat steps with remaining scallops, butter and oil. Place cookie sheet in oven and cook for about 2 minutes.

To serve, place vegetables in middle of plate and surround with scallops. Top with lemon-flavoured cream. Drizzle basil-flavoured oil around rim of plate.

WHAT TO DRINK?
A white Sauvignon from New Zealand will be perfect with this beautiful seafood dish.

If you want to prepare the Basil-Flavoured Oil ahead of time, blanch the basil leaves in boiling water and pat them dry. This will prevent the oil from darkening over time.

Tuna and Scallop Tartare

PREPARATION TIME
20 MINUTES

COOKING TIME
NONE

SERVES
4

*8 oz (225 g) red tuna or
   very fresh salmon
8 oz (225 g) very fresh scallops
1 egg yolk
¼ tsp (1 mL) Dijon mustard
1 Tbsp (15 mL) lime juice
2 Tbsp (25 mL) olive oil
1 Tbsp (15 mL) walnut oil
zest of 1 lime
2 Tbsp (25 mL) fresh chives, minced
½ tsp (2 mL) fresh dill, minced
Tabasco sauce, to taste
salt and pepper
1 shallot, finely chopped
fleur de sel
chervil for garnish*

Cut fish into small dice. Keep cold.

In bowl, mix egg yolk, mustard and lime juice. Slowly add olive and walnut oils, whisking continuously. Add lime zest, chives, dill and Tabasco sauce. Season with salt and pepper. Set aside 2 Tbsp (25 mL) of sauce to use for decoration.

In separate bowl, mix fish, sauce and shallot. Season to taste.

Place a round cookie cutter, about 2½ inches (6 cm) in diameter, on cold plate. Pour in a quarter of mixture. Press well with spoon and lift cookie cutter. Repeat steps with other 3 portions.

Drizzle the sauce around the tartare. Sprinkle with *fleur de sel* and pepper. Decorate with fresh chervil.

Serve cold with thin slices of French baguette.

WHAT TO DRINK?
A well-chilled
Sancerre or
Menetou-Salon.

I don't remember when I first became acquainted with this creature but, just like my parents, the lobster is always something I've taken for granted. I always loved it out of habit, without understanding the excitement that overtook my family every year at the beginning of May. It wasn't until the age of 20, on the beach at Ste-Anne-des-Monts (in the Gaspé region) with friends, a bonfire and an enormous pot that I finally understood the pleasure of a traditional lobster boil.

Lobster Curry

PREPARATION TIME
30 MINUTES

COOKING TIME
15 MINUTES

SERVES
4

Garam Masala
1 Tbsp (15 mL) coriander seeds
1 Tbsp (15 mL) variety of peppercorns
½ tsp (2 mL) cardamom seeds
½ tsp (2 mL) cumin seeds
¼ tsp (1 mL) ground cinnamon
¼ tsp (1 mL) ground cloves

Curry
five 1-lb (500-g) lobsters
2 Tbsp (25 mL) butter
2 onions, chopped
2 garlic cloves, chopped
½ tsp (2 mL) honey
2 tsp (10 mL) curry
1½ tsp (7 mL) garam masala
    (see recipe above)
¼ cup (50 mL) unsweetened
    coconut, grated
¼ cup (50 mL) sherry
one 14-oz (400-mL) can
    of coconut milk
1 zucchini, diced
salt

Garam Masala
Grind all spices together with mortar and pestle or in coffee mill. Keep in an airtight container in a dry place.

Curry
Cover bottom of a large saucepan with 1 inch (2.5 cm) water. Season water generously with salt and bring to boil. Add lobsters. Cook for 8 minutes from the moment water starts to boil again. After cooking, plunge lobsters into cold water. Drain. Shell lobsters, breaking tail into large pieces. Set aside.

In saucepan, melt butter. Soften onions and garlic over low heat. Season with salt. Remove from heat. In blender, reduce to a smooth paste.

Place onion paste in the saucepan with the honey, curry, garam masala and coconut. Add lobster and stir-fry for 1 minute. Deglaze with sherry. Add coconut milk and zucchini. Simmer for 2 minutes. Season to taste.

Serve with rice.

WHAT TO DRINK?
To add a fresh breeze
to this spicy dish,
nothing beats a
California
Chardonnay.

I long wondered what my neighbour was doing all winter long sitting in front of his window. One morning while we were both shovelling our driveways, I asked him, "What on earth are you doing in front of your window, Jacques?" "Salmon flies, my friend," he replied. My fishing talent stops at three framed fishing flies on the wall. But take the fish out of the water, and I'll take care of the rest. Sushi or gravlax, poached or grilled, stuffed or *en papillote*, in a mousse or aspic … I can't make a fishing fly, but I can roast a salmon, no problem. Salmon is the filet mignon of fish. In Quebec, 65 percent of people who buy fish, choose salmon. A little bit of luxury, at a reasonable price.

Cold Salmon Roast
with shrimp and vegetable stuffing

PREPARATION TIME
20 MINUTES

COOKING TIME
40 MINUTES

REFRIGERATION TIME
OVERNIGHT

SERVES
4

Sauce

½ cup (125 mL) mayonnaise
¼ cup (50 mL) sour cream
1 Tbsp (15 mL) freshly squeezed
    orange juice
grated zest of 1 lemon
1 Tbsp (15 mL) fresh mint, minced
2 Tbsp (25 mL) fresh chives, minced
salt and pepper

Salmon Roast

2 Tbsp (25 mL) butter, softened
2 cups (500 mL) fresh spinach,
    chopped
salt and pepper
1 lb (500 g) salmon fillet, skin removed
½ lb (250 g) sole fillet
1 Tbsp (15 mL) lemon juice
salt and pepper
8 large shrimps, shelled,
    cooked and chopped
    (5½ oz / 165 g, approximately)
6 asparagus, blanched

Sauce

In medium bowl, mix together all ingredients. Refrigerate and serve cold.

Salmon Roast

Place rack in centre of oven. Preheat oven to 350°F (180°C).

In skillet, melt half the butter. Add spinach and cook for about 1 minute. Season with salt and pepper. Drain. Set aside.

In a bowl, beat together the remaining butter and lemon juice and marinate the sole fillet in this mixture.

Using a sharp knife, butterfly the salmon fillet by running the knife down, but not through, the thickest part, until the fillet opens flat like a book. Place the opened fillet on a piece of parchment paper. Place the marinated sole fillet lengthwise down the centre of the salmon and sprinkle with salt and pepper. Next, add the layer of spinach and then the shrimp. Finally, place the asparagus lengthwise down the centre.

Use the edge of the parchment to lift and roll the salmon around the stuffing, keeping the parchment on the outside of the roll. Then wrap the bundle in foil and place in an ovenproof dish.

Cook in oven for about 40 minutes or until meat thermometer reaches 135°F (58°C).

Cool and then refrigerate overnight. Remove parchment paper. Slice and serve cold with sauce.

WHAT TO DRINK?
A well-chilled
Chablis.

Semi-Cooked Tuna Steak
with almonds and mashed ginger butternut squash

PREPARATION TIME
30 MINUTES

COOKING TIME
1 HOUR, 25 MINUTES

SERVES
4

Mashed Butternut Squash

1 large butternut squash
3 Tbsp (45 mL) butter
1 Tbsp (15 mL) fresh ginger, grated
pinch of nutmeg
salt and pepper

Semi-Cooked Tuna with Almonds

1 egg
1 cup (250 mL) ground almonds
4 tsp (20 mL) ground ginger
4 tuna steaks, 1 inch (2.5 cm) thick
olive oil
12 fresh chive stems, to decorate

Basil-Flavoured Emulsion

¼ cup (50 mL) fresh basil, minced
¼ cup (50 mL) olive oil
1 tsp (5 mL) white wine vinegar
¼ cup (50 mL) water

Mashed Butternut Squash

Place rack in centre of oven. Preheat oven to 350°F (180°C).

Cut squash in half, lengthwise, and seed. Place halves on cookie sheet, rounded side up.

Cook in oven for about 1 hour, depending on the size of the squash. Cool. Remove flesh with a spoon and mash with butter, ginger and nutmeg. Season with salt and pepper. Set aside.

Semi-Cooked Tuna with Almonds

In deep plate, beat egg lightly. In another plate, mix almonds and ginger. Dip tuna pieces into egg, then coat with almond mixture.

In skillet, grill tuna in olive oil until crust is golden on both sides. Tuna steaks should be rare on the inside.

Basil-Flavoured Emulsion

In blender, process basil, olive oil, vinegar and water until mixture is smooth.

To serve, garnish middle of each plate with mashed squash. Place tuna at an angle, resting on squash. Spread emulsion all around tuna, and decorate with chives.

WHAT TO DRINK?
A cheerful
California
Pinot Noir.

You may prepare the emulsion with coriander, sorrel or any other herb of your choice. Ideally, it should be made at the last minute.

easy
entertaining

Meat and Poultry

Lamb Chops
with mint and green pea couscous

PREPARATION TIME
30 MINUTES

MARINATING TIME
2 TO 4 HOURS

COOKING TIME
8 MINUTES

SERVES
3 TO 4

Lamb Chops

¼ cup (50 mL) olive oil
3 Tbsp (45 mL) fresh thyme,
    leaves only
zest and juice of 1 lemon
12 lamb chops, fat trimmed
¼ cup (50 mL) flour
1 egg, beaten
¾ cup (175 mL) pistachios, finely
    chopped in processor
salt and pepper
3 Tbsp (45 mL) olive oil

Couscous

1 onion, finely chopped
1 garlic clove, finely chopped
3 Tbsp (45 mL) olive oil
1 cup (250 mL) frozen green
    peas, thawed
1½ cups (375 mL) couscous
1½ cups (375 mL) chicken stock,
    boiling hot
3 Tbsp (45 mL) fresh mint, minced

Lemon Emulsion with Mint

⅓ cup (75 mL) olive oil
1 Tbsp (15 mL) lemon juice
1 garlic clove, finely chopped
2 Tbsp (25 mL) fresh mint,
    finely chopped
salt and pepper

Lamb Chops

In large bowl, mix oil, thyme, zest and lemon juice. Add lamb chops, mix and marinate for 2 to 4 hours in refrigerator.

Couscous

In saucepan, brown onion and garlic in olive oil. Add peas and continue cooking for 2 minutes. Remove from heat. Add couscous and stock. Mix. Cover and let stand for 5 minutes. Loosen grains with fork. Add mint and season to taste. Keep warm.

Lemon Emulsion with Mint

In small blender or with a whisk, mix olive oil, lemon juice, garlic and mint. Season with salt and pepper.

Place rack in centre of oven. Preheat oven to 350°F (180°C).

Pat lamb chops dry and dredge with flour. Dip chops into beaten egg and cover with pistachios. Season with salt and pepper.

In large skillet, heat olive oil. Add chops to skillet and sear over high heat, 30 seconds per side. Place on cookie sheet and cook in oven for 6 to 7 minutes for rare meat.

To serve, place couscous in middle of plate. Place 3 chops onto each plate and drizzle lemon emulsion with mint over the top.

AS FOR WINE?
A Cabernet
Sauvignon
from Chile.

Flank Steak
with shallots and homemade fries

PREPARATION TIME
10 MINUTES

MARINATING TIME
2 TO 4 HOURS

COOKING TIME
15 MINUTES

SERVES
4

4 flank steaks, 5 oz (150 g) each
butter

Marinade
2 garlic cloves, chopped
3 sprigs fresh thyme, leaves only
2 Tbsp (25 mL) olive oil
1 cup (250 mL) red wine
salt and pepper

Shallot Sauce
⅔ cup (150 mL) shallots, minced
⅔ cup (150 mL) white wine
1 Tbsp (15 mL) white wine vinegar
¼ cup (50 mL) cold butter, diced
salt and pepper

Homemade Fries
a few russet (Idaho) potatoes
peanut oil, canola oil or non-extra
    virgin olive oil, for frying
coarse salt or fleur de sel

Using sharp knife, cut a crisscross pattern on both sides of each steak.

Marinade
In large bowl, mix garlic, thyme, oil and wine. Season with salt and pepper. Add steaks and cover well with marinade. Cover bowl and marinate in refrigerator for 2 to 4 hours.

Shallot Sauce
In small saucepan, cook shallots in wine and vinegar over low heat for about 5 minutes.

Beat in butter, one piece at a time, making sure each piece melts before adding the next. Sauce must not boil. Season with salt and pepper. Keep warm.

Remove steaks from marinade. Drain. In medium skillet, sear steaks in butter over high heat (see note below). Serve steaks raw or rare, topped with shallot sauce, with homemade fries.

Homemade Fries
Peel potatoes or wash without peeling. Cut into matchsticks. Soak in hot water for about 10 minutes. Drain and pat dry.

Preheat oil in deep fryer to 350°F (180°C). Dip fries into oil, a few at a time, and fry for 5 minutes. Drain and keep in strainer (you may do this several hours ahead of time).

Increase fryer heat to 375°F (190°C). Dip fries into oil a second time and cook until deep golden. Pat dry on paper towel. Season with salt.

AS FOR WINE?
A Côtes-du-Rhône
Villages.

Flank steak is a classic cut for French butchers. Request it from your butcher in advance because you can't always find it pre-packaged. This is one of the most economical cuts of beef to grill. For tender steak, sear over high heat and serve raw or rare.

Pork Medallions
with raspberries

PREPARATION TIME
10 MINUTES

COOKING TIME
15 MINUTES

SERVES
4

2 pork tenderloins
flour
1 Tbsp (15 mL) olive oil
2 Tbsp (25 mL) butter
1 onion, finely chopped
1 garlic clove, finely chopped
1 tsp (5 mL) honey
1 tsp (5 mL) raspberry vinegar
½ cup (125 mL) chicken stock
1 cup (250 mL) fresh raspberries
salt and pepper

Place rack in centre of oven. Preheat oven to 350°F (180°C).

Slice each tenderloin into 6 medallions. Flatten lightly and flour each one.

In ovenproof skillet, heat oil and butter. Add medallions and brown over high heat for about 1 minute per side. Season with salt and pepper. Remove medallions from skillet and set aside.

In same skillet, soften onion and garlic, this time on medium heat. Add honey and cook for 1 minute. Deglaze with vinegar. Add stock and half of raspberries. Cook for 1 to 2 minutes.

Return medallions to skillet. Cook in oven for about 10 minutes. Add remaining raspberries. Season to taste.

To serve, cover medallions with sauce. Serve with asparagus.

SOME WINE?
A nice red from Val de Loire will blend perfectly with the fruity perfume of raspberries and the delicate tenderloins. Choose a Chinon or Bourgueil.

Rib Roast
with Béarnaise sauce

PREPARATION TIME
15 MINUTES

COOKING TIME
1 HOUR, 45 MINUTES

SERVES
6 TO 8

one 5-lb (2.2-kg) rib roast
3 Tbsp (45 mL) Dijon mustard
salt and pepper

Béarnaise Sauce
¼ cup (50 mL) dry white wine
3 Tbsp (45 mL) white wine vinegar
½ cup (125 mL) shallots,
    finely chopped
1 Tbsp (15 mL) fresh tarragon, minced
3 egg yolks
¾ cup (175 mL) salted butter,
    melted and cooled
pepper

Place rack in centre of oven. Preheat oven to 375°F (190°C).

Place beef in roasting pan. Spread mustard on meat with your hands. Season generously with salt and pepper and insert a meat thermometer into the thickest part of roast.

Cook roast in oven for 15 minutes, then reduce heat to 325°F (170°C). Continue cooking for about 1 hour and 30 minutes. Remove roast from oven when meat thermometer reaches 3 to 4 degrees less than recommended temperature, which is 150°F (57°C) for rare meat, 155°F (68°C) for medium, and 170°F (77°C) for well done. Wrap roast in aluminum foil and let stand for about 10 minutes before slicing.

Béarnaise Sauce
In small saucepan, bring wine, vinegar, shallots and tarragon to a boil. Reduce until only 2 Tbsp (25 mL) of liquid remains. Remove from heat and cool.

Add egg yolks and beat over low heat until mixture thickens.

Remove saucepan from heat. Pour butter over egg yolks, beating until mixture thickens. Season to taste. Keep warm over double boiler.

Slice roast and serve with sauce, a salad and potatoes.

A LITTLE WINE ?
A full-bodied red wine, such as a Medoc, will be perfect.

I must admit that stewed dishes don't interest me. This Flemish-Style Carbonnade is the exception. It has both a sweet and salty side that I enjoy … particularly with mashed potatoes.

Flemish-Style Carbonnade

PREPARATION TIME
15 MINUTES

COOKING TIME
2 HOURS

SERVES
6 TO 8

2 ½ lb (1.2 kg) slices of beef, cut in round part (round steak)
¼ cup (50 mL) flour
3 Tbsp (45 mL) vegetable oil
¼ cup (50 mL) butter
6 onions, sliced
2 bottles (341 mL each) microbrewery beer, pale ale or other
3 Tbsp (45 mL) honey
3 Tbsp (45 mL) Dijon mustard
2 Tbsp (25 mL) red wine vinegar
2 bay leaves
1 tsp (5 mL) dried thyme
salt and pepper

Place rack in centre of oven. Preheat oven to 375°F (190°C).

Flour beef. In large ovenproof saucepan, heat oil and half of butter. Add beef and brown, a few slices at a time. Season with salt and pepper. Set aside. If necessary, scrape bottom of saucepan to remove accumulated flour.

In same saucepan, brown onions in remaining butter. Add reserved meat and remaining ingredients. Season with salt and pepper. Bring to a boil.

Cook in oven, uncovered, for about 1 hour and 45 minutes. Season to taste. Serve with mashed vegetables.

A LITTLE WINE?
Nothing is better with this dish than a good classified red wine such as Bordeaux Supérieur.

Here's a simple way of being exotic in the kitchen without using any complicated cooking equipment. A grill, aluminum foil and a mixture of good teas are all you need. This ancient Chinese technique allows you to smoke chicken in spiced tea vapours, giving it an original taste; it's a welcome change from the usual barbecue chicken.

Tea-Smoked Chicken

PREPARATION TIME
15 MINUTES

COOKING TIME
1 HOUR, 20 MINUTES

SERVES
4

½ cup (125 mL) long grain rice
2 Tbsp (25 mL) brown sugar
2 star anises, ground
½ tsp (2 mL) five-spice powder
¾ cup (180 mL) Gunpowder
    green tea
1 piece of orange peel
4 chicken breasts (bone in),
    or 1 small chicken
salt and pepper
soy sauce

Tea Sauce
1 shallot, chopped
2 Tbsp (25 mL) butter
2 Tbsp (25 mL) flour
1 tsp (5 mL) Earl Grey tea leaves
1 cup (250 mL) chicken stock
¼ cup (50 mL) 15% cream
salt and pepper

Place rack on bottom level of oven. Preheat oven to 350°F (180°C).

Remove rack from roasting pan. Cover bottom of roasting pan with aluminum foil. Mix together all ingredients, except for chicken, soy sauce, salt and pepper. Replace rack.

Place roasting pan in oven for 10 to 15 minutes, until mixture starts to smoke. Place chicken on rack. Season with salt and pepper. Cover completely with aluminum foil in order to obtain airtight cooking. Cook in oven for about 55 minutes.

Uncover chicken and baste with soy sauce. Continue cooking for about 15 minutes, or until the juices run clear. Cooking time will be longer if chicken is whole. Serve chicken with tea sauce.

Tea Sauce
In small saucepan, soften shallot in butter. Sprinkle with flour. Mix and cook for about 1 minute over medium-high heat. Add Earl Grey tea and chicken stock. Cook while stirring until mixture thickens. Add cream and reduce for 1 minute. Season with salt and pepper.

WHAT TO DRINK?
A white Graves
(Bordeaux) or
a white Sauvignon
from California.

129

Five-Spice Sweetbreads

PREPARATION TIME
20 MINUTES

COOKING TIME
15 MINUTES

SERVES
4

1¾ lb (875 g) sweetbreads
½ cup (125 mL) flour
6 Tbsp (90 mL) duck fat or butter
1 shallot, finely chopped
2 garlic cloves, chopped
1 Tbsp (15 mL) five-spice powder
1 Tbsp (15 mL) honey
1 tsp (5 mL) white wine vinegar
1 cup (250 mL) muscat wine

In saucepan of simmering salted water, poach sweetbreads for 5 minutes, then dip into ice-cold water. Drain well. Remove membrane, venules (small veins) and fat that cover sweetbreads. Cut each sweetbread into pieces or thin cutlets. Flour.

In skillet, heat 2 Tbsp (30 mL) of the duck fat or butter. Brown sweetbread pieces, in batches, using an additional 2 Tbsp (30 mL) of fat or butter, keeping 2 Tbsp (30 mL) in reserve. Season with salt and pepper. Keep warm.

In same skillet, brown shallot, garlic and five-spice powder in remaining duck fat. Add honey and caramelize for 1 minute. Deglaze with vinegar, then with muscat. Reduce until mixture becomes syrupy. Return warm sweetbreads to the skillet. Season to taste.

Serve with Mashed Celeriac with Spinach (recipe page 78).

A LITTLE WINE?
Consider two
sumptuous wines
from Burgundy:
a Meursault or a
Corton-Charlemagne.

You can buy duck fat in a butcher shop or delicatessen. I accumulate it and keep it in airtight containers in the freezer. With the same fat required for this recipe, you can make confit with duck, pork tenderloin or turkey legs all year long. You only have to filter the fat while it's still hot. I can tell you that confit keeps getting better every time, the fat having gained more flavour.

Turkey Confit

PREPARATION TIME
10 MINUTES

WAITING TIME
24 HOURS

COOKING TIME
3 HOURS

SERVES
6

Seasoned Salt
¼ cup (50 mL) coarse salt
2 bay leaves, crushed
4 juniper berries
2 Tbsp (25 mL) coriander seeds
1 sprig fresh thyme, leaves only
2 tsp (10 mL) pink peppercorns
2 cloves

2 turkey legs, 2 lb (1 kg) each
8 cups (2 L) duck fat, approximately

In small bowl, mix coarse salt, bay leaves, juniper berries, coriander seeds, thyme, pepper and cloves.

Place turkey legs in large ovenproof saucepan. Sprinkle each leg with 4 Tbsp (20 mL) of seasoned salt. Cover and refrigerate for 24 hours.

Place rack in centre of oven. Preheat oven to 275°F (140°C).

Rinse turkey legs and pat dry. Clean saucepan and return poultry to pan.

In another saucepan, melt duck fat over low heat. Pour melted duck fat over turkey, covering well. Put lid on saucepan and cook in oven for 3 hours, or until meat detaches easily from its bones.

Debone turkey legs and serve on bed of mesclun (mixture of young lettuces) tossed with a simple salad dressing such as my French salad dressing (page 71).

AS FOR WINE?
A Malbec from
Argentina.

As with duck confit, turkey confit can be easily frozen. It will keep for up to one week in the refrigerator, in its cooking fat.

Indian-Style Chicken

3 Tbsp (45 mL) olive oil
2 onions, chopped
3 garlic cloves, chopped
1 Tbsp (15 mL) fresh ginger, chopped
1 tsp (5 mL) ground cumin
1 tsp (5 mL) medium curry powder
1 lb (500 g) chicken breasts,
    boned, skinned and cubed
    in 1-inch (2.5 cm) pieces
salt and pepper
1 cup (250 mL) coconut milk
2 plum tomatoes, diced and seeded
¼ cup (50 mL) fresh coriander,
    minced

In large skillet, heat olive oil. Brown onion and garlic with ginger, cumin and curry. Add chicken and cook for 5 minutes over high heat, stirring frequently. Season with salt and pepper.

Add coconut milk and tomatoes to skillet. Continue cooking for 5 minutes. Add coriander. Season to taste.

Serve with basmati or biryani rice.

PREPARATION TIME
15 MINUTES

COOKING TIME
12 MINUTES

SERVES
4

WHAT TO DRINK?
A nice white wine
full of sun: Viognier
from Languedoc
or from Rhône
or Alsatian
Gewürztraminer.

Biryani Rice

2 onions, sliced
3 Tbsp (45 mL) olive oil
4 garlic cloves, chopped
1 cup (250 mL) basmati rice
1½ tsp (7 mL) curry powder
1 Tbsp (15 mL) grated fresh ginger
2 cups (500 mL) chicken stock
1½ cups (375 mL) cauliflower pieces
⅓ cup (75 mL) carrots, diced
    in small pieces
⅓ cup (75 mL) frozen green peas
⅓ cup (75 mL) dried raisins
⅓ cup (75 mL) whole pistachios
salt and pepper

In medium-large saucepan, slowly cook onions in olive oil until golden. Add garlic and continue cooking for 2 minutes. Add rice, curry and ginger. Mix well. Add remaining ingredients and mix well.

Bring to a boil. Reduce heat to very low. Cover and cook for about 20 minutes, without stirring. Liquid should be completely absorbed. Remove from heat and serve.

PREPARATION TIME
25 MINUTES

COOKING TIME
30 MINUTES

SERVES
4 TO 6

I remember moving into our first home. There was no way I'd offer beer and pizza to our friends who had volunteered to help. The evening before, after we finished packing, Brigitte and I prepared osso bucco. After the move, we all sat down at the table around the steaming dish, with a few bottles of red wine. I'll never forget the aromas of that evening.

Osso Bucco
veal shanks with tomatoes and white wine

PREPARATION TIME
30 MINUTES

COOKING TIME
2 HOURS

SERVES
4

flour
4 pieces of veal shanks, approximately
    2 inches (5 cm) thick
olive oil
2 onions, chopped
1½ cups (375 mL) dry white wine
1 can (19 oz / 540 mL) tomatoes
2 celery stalks, chopped
2 carrots, chopped
4 garlic cloves, chopped
2 Tbsp (30 mL) tomato paste
1 cup (250 mL) beef stock
1 bay leaf
1 tsp (5 mL) dried thyme
salt and pepper

Gremolata
zest of 2 grated lemons
¼ cup (50 mL) fresh parsley,
    finely chopped
1 garlic clove, finely chopped
pepper

Place rack in centre of oven. Preheat to 350°F (180°C).

Flour veal shanks. In large casserole dish, brown veal on both sides, in olive oil. Season with salt and pepper. Remove from casserole dish and set aside.

Wipe casserole dish with paper towel. Add oil as needed and cook onions until tender but not browned. Deglaze with white wine.

Add tomatoes, shanks and remaining ingredients. Salt lightly and add pepper.

Bring to a boil, cover and cook in oven for 45 minutes. Then reduce oven temperature to 325°F (160°C) and continue cooking for about 1 hour. Season to taste.

Serve with gremolata, orzo and zucchini ribbons.

Gremolata
Mix all ingredients in small bowl.

AS FOR WINE?
A generous
Italian red,
such as Barolo.

Chicken Supremes
stuffed with ricotta and dried tomatoes

PREPARATION TIME
30 MINUTES

COOKING TIME
15 MINUTES

SERVES
4

¼ cup (50 mL) dried tomatoes in oil,
    drained and finely chopped
½ cup (125 mL) ricotta cheese
1 egg white
¼ cup (50 mL) fresh basil, minced
1 green onion, finely chopped
2 chicken breasts, halved,
    skinned and deboned
4 slices prosciutto ham
1 Tbsp (15 mL) butter
1 Tbsp (15 mL) olive oil

Pasta with Tomatoes and Cheese
¾ lb (375 g) tagliatelle pasta
½ cup (125 mL) ricotta cheese
2 Tbsp (25 mL) olive oil
3 plum tomatoes, seeded and diced
¼ cup (50 mL) fresh flat
    parsley, minced
½ cup (125 mL) chicken stock
salt and pepper

Place rack in centre of oven. Preheat oven
to 375°F (190°C).

In bowl, mix dried tomatoes, ricotta, egg white,
basil and green onion.

On clean work surface, butterfly the breast halves.
To do this, slice each breast in half at thickest part
without separating it completely, then open like a
book. Spread dried tomato stuffing down the centre
of each breast. Close each breast on itself. Wrap with
a slice of prosciutto ham and attach with a toothpick.

In large ovenproof skillet, heat butter and oil. Add
chicken, browning on all sides. Cook in oven for
5 to 6 minutes, or until chicken is cooked through
and juices run clear.

Pasta with Tomatoes and Cheese
Meanwhile, in large saucepan, cook pasta in boiling
salted water. Drain, reserving a little water. Return
pasta to saucepan. Add remaining ingredients. Add a
little reserved cooking water to saucepan to moisten
pasta, if necessary. Season with salt and pepper.

Serve chicken with the pasta.

AS FOR WINE?
An Italian classic
such as a
Valpolicella
Classico Superiore.

Rack of Veal Provençal

PREPARATION TIME
15 MINUTES

COOKING TIME
1 HOUR, 30 MINUTES

SERVES
6

10 garlic cloves, chopped
¼ cup (50 mL) butter, softened
1 rack of veal (4 lb / 2 kg), 6
    ribs (see note below)
12 plum tomatoes, peeled,
    seeded and halved
12 cipollini onions (small sweet
    Italian onions) or 24 small
    pickling onions, peeled
3 zucchini, diced
1 sprig fresh thyme, leaves only
1 sprig fresh rosemary, leaves only
3 bay leaves
1 cup (250 mL) chicken stock
½ cup (125 mL) white wine
2 Tbsp (25 mL) fresh flat
    parsley, minced
salt and pepper

Place rack in centre of oven. Preheat oven to 450°F (230°C).

In small bowl, mix two garlic cloves with butter. Spread on meat. Season generously with salt and pepper. Set aside.

Place remaining ingredients, except parsley, in 13- × 9-inch (33- × 23-cm) pan. Season with salt and pepper. Place meat on top of vegetables.

Cook for 15 minutes, then reduce heat to 375°F (190°C) and continue cooking for about 1 hour and 15 minutes. Remove meat from oven when temperature on meat thermometer reaches 145°F (63°C).

Remove veal from oven, wrap in aluminum foil and let stand for 15 minutes. Sprinkle parsley over vegetables and keep warm. Slice veal and serve coated with vegetable mix and stock.

A rack of veal is a delicious cut of meat, but expensive. When ordering, ask your butcher to trim it and saw the bone under the ribs for you. You may also make this recipe with a rack of pork, which is more affordable. Note that the recommended internal temperature for cooked pork is 158°F (70°C).

AS FOR WINE?

You'll appreciate the fineness of this rack of veal by harmonizing it with a red Côtes de Provence.

Pork Roast
with apples and maple syrup

PREPARATION TIME
20 MINUTES

COOKING TIME
1 HOUR

SERVES
6

flour
1 tenderloin roast (2 ½ lb / 1.2 kg)
3 Tbsp (45 mL) butter
3 Tbsp (45 mL) maple syrup
1 onion
3 Tbsp (45 mL) Dijon mustard
1 cup (250 mL) white wine
3 Cortland apples, peeled, seeded
    and quartered
1 cup (250 mL) chicken stock
½ tsp (2.5 mL) dried tarragon
1 bay leaf
¼ cup (50 mL) 35% cream
salt and pepper

Place rack in centre of oven. Preheat oven to 350°F (180°C). Flour roast on all sides.

In ovenproof saucepan, melt butter. Add roast and brown on all sides on high heat. Add maple syrup and caramelize for 2 to 3 minutes. Remove roast from saucepan. Set aside.

In same saucepan, brown onion. Return roast to saucepan and baste with mustard. Add wine and reduce for 2 minutes. Add apples, stock, tarragon and bay leaf. Season with salt and pepper. Bring to a boil.

Cook in oven for about 45 minutes, or until internal temperature on meat thermometer reaches 3 to 4 degrees less than recommended temperature (158°F / 70°C). Remove from saucepan and cover with aluminum foil. Let stand for 10 minutes on counter.

Meanwhile, return saucepan to heat. Pour cream into saucepan, stirring, and bring to boil. Reduce by half. Season to taste. Cut roast into thin slices, cover with sauce and serve with mashed vegetables (page 78).

A LITTLE WINE ?
Pork and apples
go very well with a
white wine such as an
Australian Chardonnay
or with a light red wine.

Several recipes, such as this one, require demi-glace sauce. It's a sauce that, in a nutshell, is a reduction of a brown stock that's simmered for about 15 hours. It's used to give "body" to a sauce. Few people attempt to make one at home because of the lengthy time required. Store-bought demi-glace is always an interesting alternative, but pay careful attention to the quality, which varies. The best option is homemade demi-glace purchased at the butcher's or a delicatessen. I've also tested several pre-packaged dry mixes, and Knorr's, even though a bit salty, is worth trying.

Leg of Lamb
with red wine and herbs

PREPARATION TIME
15 MINUTES

MARINATING TIME
24 HOURS

COOKING TIME
40 MINUTES

SERVES
4

Marinade
1 cup (250 mL) red wine
1 Tbsp (15 mL) red wine vinegar
1 Tbsp (15 mL) whisky
3 Tbsp (45 mL) vegetable oil
1 Tbsp (15 mL) honey
1 Tbsp (15 mL) Dijon mustard
2 shallots, finely chopped
3 garlic cloves, peeled and crushed
1 sprig fresh thyme
3 fresh sage leaves
salt and pepper

Leg of Lamb
1 leg of lamb, boned (2 lb / 1 kg)
1 sprig fresh rosemary
1 shallot, finely chopped
1 Tbsp (15 mL) butter
1 cup (250 mL) demi-glace sauce

In large bowl, mix all ingredients for the marinade. Place leg of lamb in it, cover and marinate for 24 hours in refrigerator.

Place rack in centre of oven. Preheat oven to 400°F (200°C).

Remove leg from marinade. Set aside half of the marinade and discard the rest. Place rosemary sprig on the inside of the leg. Close leg, tie and place in a pan. Pour reserved marinade onto the leg. Season with salt and pepper.

Cook in oven for 15 minutes, then reduce temperature to 375°F (190°C). Continue cooking for about 25 minutes. Remove meat when meat thermometer reaches 145°F (63°C).

Remove leg from pan. Wrap in aluminum foil and place on cutting board. Let stand for 10 to 15 minutes. The thermometer should reach about 155°F (68°C) for rare meat.

Filter cooking juices through strainer. Set aside.

In the same saucepan, brown shallot in butter on high heat. Add cooking juices from meat and reduce until syrupy. Add demi-glace sauce and cook for 1 minute. Season to taste.

Slice leg of lamb and cover with sauce. Serve with Overlooked Root Vegetables in Glaze (recipe page 75).

AS FOR WINE?
A beautiful and full-bodied red would be excellent. Why not a Châteauneuf-du-Pape or a Gigondas?

Thai-Style Veal Scaloppini

Sauce

¾ cup (175 mL) 15% cream
2 Tbsp (25 mL) unsweetened
   coconut, grated
1 Tbsp (15 mL) lime juice
¼ cup (50 mL) fresh coriander, minced
salt and pepper

Pasta

7 oz (200 g) soba noodles
   (see note below)
3 Tbsp (45 mL) non-toasted sesame oil
½ cup (125 mL) snow peas,
   cut into matchsticks
½ sweet red pepper, cut into
   matchsticks
2 Tbsp (25 mL) black or white
   roasted sesame seeds
salt and pepper

Scaloppini

12 scaloppini (small veal cutlets)
2 eggs, beaten
1 cup (250 mL) unsalted peanuts,
   finely chopped in food processor
¼ cup (50 mL) peanut oil
salt and pepper

Sauce

In small saucepan, bring cream, coconut and lime juice to boil. Reduce by half. Add coriander. Season with salt and pepper. Keep warm.

Pasta

Cook noodles in boiling salted water for 4 to 5 minutes. Drain and set aside.

In skillet, heat sesame oil. Add snow peas and sweet pepper and brown for 2 minutes. In bowl, mix noodles, vegetables and sesame seeds. Season with salt and pepper. Keep warm.

Scaloppini

Season scaloppini with salt and pepper. Dip into beaten eggs and coat with peanuts.

In skillet, heat peanut oil. Add scaloppini, a few at a time, browning each side.

Serve scaloppini with pasta and sauce.

AS FOR WINE?
For an agreeable
contrast with
Thai spices,
try an Alsatian
Gewürztraminer.

Soba noodles are pasta made of buckwheat and very popular in Asian countries. In Canada, you can find them in Asian grocery stores, in an increasing number of supermarkets and in natural food stores. You can recognize them by their brownish colour. During the summer, I enjoy serving them cold with soy sauce, sesame oil, red sweet peppers, green onions and snow peas.

143

Duck and Potato Hash

PREPARATION TIME
40 MINUTES

COOKING TIME
3 HOURS, 20 MINUTES

SERVES
6

1 duck, about 5½ lb (2 kg)
2 cups (500 mL) red wine
1 cup (250 mL) duck
    or chicken stock
1 onion, chopped
4 garlic cloves, peeled and
    quartered
2 sprigs thyme
1 bay leaf
salt and pepper
1 onion, finely chopped
1 Tbsp (15 mL) butter
1 Tbsp (15 mL) bread crumbs
1 Tbsp (15 mL) grated
    Parmigiano Reggiano
1 Tbsp (15 mL) fresh chives, minced

Mashed Potatoes

6 cups (1.5 L) Yukon Gold potatoes,
    peeled and cut into pieces
    (about 9 medium
    potatoes)
½ cup (125 mL) grated cheddar cheese
2 Tbsp (25 mL) butter
¾ cup (175 mL) milk, approximately
1 egg yolk
1 Tbsp (15 mL) fresh flat
    parsley, minced
salt and pepper

Place rack in centre of oven. Preheat oven to 350°F (180°C).

Place duck in large ovenproof saucepan and cover with water. Bring to a boil. Reduce heat and simmer for 30 minutes.

Drain and return duck to saucepan. Add wine, stock, onion, garlic, thyme and bay leaf. Season with salt and pepper. Cook in oven for about 2 hours and 30 minutes, or until meat thermometer reaches 180°F (82°C).

Remove duck from saucepan and cool. Filter cooking juice through strainer. Discard garlic, onion and herbs. Let fat come to the surface of cooking juice; remove fat. You'll get 1½ cups (375 mL) degreased liquid.

Debone duck and cut into little pieces. Set aside.

Mashed Potatoes

One half hour before end of cooking time, cook potatoes in boiling salted water. Drain well and mash with cheese, butter, milk, egg and parsley. Season with salt and pepper. Keep warm.

Assembly

In saucepan, brown chopped onion in butter. Add duck and its cooking juice. Season to taste.

Place duck preparation in a 13- × 9-inch (33- × 23-cm) pan or in 6 ramekins, 5 inches (13 cm) in diameter. Cover with mashed potatoes. Sprinkle with bread crumbs and Parmesan cheese. Cook in oven for 15 minutes, then brown under broil. Sprinkle with minced chives and serve.

A LITTLE WINE?
Why not a good California Zinfandel?

Deer Steak
with mushroom and roasted hazelnut sauce

PREPARATION TIME
10 MINUTES

WAITING TIME
20 MINUTES

COOKING TIME
15 MINUTES

SERVES
4

*1 cup (250 mL) dried boletus
    mushrooms, about two
    ¾-oz (20-g) packages*
1 Tbsp (15 mL) vegetable oil
3 Tbsp (45 mL) butter
4 deer steaks
salt and pepper
1 shallot, chopped
1 garlic clove, chopped
*¼ cup (50 mL) roasted
    hazelnuts, chopped*
1 tsp (5 mL) honey
1 tsp (5 mL) red wine vinegar
¼ cup (50 mL) red wine
*1 cup (250 mL) demi-glace sauce
    (see introduction to page 141)*

Place mushrooms in bowl and cover with 1 cup (250 mL) boiling water. Let stand for about 20 minutes. Drain. Reserve water.

In skillet, heat oil and 1 Tbsp (15 mL) butter. Add steaks and cook over high heat, until done to taste. Season with salt and pepper. Keep warm.

Place 1 Tbsp (15 mL) butter in skillet and brown shallot and garlic. Add hazelnuts and mushrooms. Continue cooking for 2 minutes. Season with salt and pepper.

Add honey and vinegar. Deglaze with red wine and reserved mushroom water. Reduce by three quarters. Add demi-glace. Bring to a boil. Remove from heat. Add remaining butter. Season to taste.

Place steaks on four plates and cover with sauce. Serve with mashed vegetables (recipes page 78).

AS FOR WINE?

You'll honour this beautiful red meat with a sumptuous Bordeaux such as a Lalande-de-Pomerol or a Pomerol.

American-Style Chicken

PREPARATION TIME
15 MINUTES

COOKING TIME
**FROM 1 HOUR TO
1 HOUR, 30 MINUTES**

SERVES
4

6 slices bacon, thinly sliced
4 cups (1 L) mushrooms, quartered
4 plum tomatoes, seeded and diced
salt and pepper
2 small or 1 large chicken
¼ cup (50 mL) butter, softened
2 Tbsp (25 mL) Dijon mustard
¼ cup (50 mL) bread crumbs
2 Tbsp (25 mL) paprika

Place rack in centre of oven. Preheat oven to 375°F (190°C). Cover bottom of deep cookie sheet with parchment paper.

In medium skillet, brown bacon. Add mushrooms and stir-fry until they've lost all their liquid. Remove from heat and add tomatoes. Season with salt and pepper. Set aside.

On cutting board, open chicken by placing on its back, driving a chef's knife through the middle and splitting the backbones. You can ask your butcher to do this.

Place chicken flat on cookie sheet. Spread butter and mustard on it and sprinkle with bread crumbs and paprika. Season with salt and pepper.

Cook in oven for about 50 minutes for small chicken and between 1 hour and 1 hour and 15 minutes for a large one. Add mushroom garnish all around the chicken and continue cooking for about 15 minutes or until meat thermometer reaches 180°F (82°C).

Carve chicken and serve with mushroom garnish, rice or mashed potatoes.

AS FOR WINE?
A light red:
vintage from
Beaujolais such
as a Fleurie
or a Morgon.

Duck Magrets
breast cutlets with vodka and cranberries

PREPARATION TIME
10 MINUTES

COOKING TIME
25 MINUTES

SERVES
4

2 duck breasts
2 shallots, finely chopped
½ cup (125 mL) dried cranberries
⅓ cup (75 mL) vodka
juice of 2 oranges
¾ cup (180 mL) fresh or frozen
    cranberries
1 cup (250 mL) demi-glace sauce
    (see introduction to page 141)
salt and pepper

Place oven rack in middle of oven.
Preheat oven to 350°F (180°C).

Using a sharp knife, make crisscross pattern in fat
of each breast without cutting meat. In ovenproof
skillet, brown breasts, fat side down, for approximately
10 minutes over low heat. Season with salt and
pepper. Drain excess fat from skillet. Turn breasts
over and cook in oven for approximately 7 minutes,
for pink-coloured meat. Set the meat aside.

In same skillet, cook shallots and dried cranberries
until soft. Deglaze with vodka and reduce by half.
Add orange juice and fresh cranberries. Cook for
2 minutes. Add demi-glace sauce. Bring to a boil
and season to taste.

Slice breasts, top with sauce and serve with
Overlooked Root Vegetables in Glaze (recipe page 75).

AS FOR WINE?
A red Burgundy
will mesh perfectly with
duck breast and
its berries.

149

a sweet touch

"I can do it too, Daddy!"

CLÉMENCE, 4 YEARS OLD

Desserts

Double-Chocolate Eclairs

PREPARATION TIME
1 HOUR

COOKING TIME
1 HOUR

WAITING TIME
3 TO 4 HOURS

SERVES
8

Choux Pastry

½ cup (125 mL) water
¼ cup (50 mL) unsalted butter
½ cup (125 mL) flour
2 eggs

Custard

¼ cup (50 mL) sugar
1 tsp (5 mL) vanilla extract
2 eggs
2 Tbsp (25 mL) flour
1 cup (250 mL) milk, warmed
4 oz (100 g) white
    chocolate, chopped
3 oz (75 g) semi-sweet
    chocolate, melted

Choux Pastry

In saucepan, bring water and butter to a boil. Remove from heat. Add flour all at once and mix well using wooden spoon, until dough forms a ball and detaches from the side of bowl.

Cool for a few minutes. Add eggs, one at a time, stirring briskly between each addition until dough becomes smooth and well mixed.

Place rack in centre of oven. Preheat oven to 375°F (19°C). Butter cookie sheet and cover with parchment paper.

Using pastry bag filled with dough, form eclairs of about 3 inches (8 cm) in length on cookie sheet.

Bake eclairs in oven until they're golden, about 30 minutes. Slice eclairs lengthwise to allow steam to escape, then return them to the oven for a short time to dry slightly. Remove from oven and cool.

Custard

In saucepan, before heating, beat sugar, vanilla and eggs until mixture becomes white. Add flour and cream until mixture is smooth and well-mixed. Add warm milk and white chocolate. Stir over low heat until thickened.

Remove custard from heat and cover with plastic wrap. Refrigerate for 3 to 4 hours.

Using pastry bag, fill eclairs with custard. With a spoon, coat top of eclairs with melted semi-sweet chocolate. Refrigerate.

Panna Cotta
with strawberry coulis

PREPARATION TIME
10 MINUTES

COOKING TIME
10 MINUTES

WAITING TIME
6 HOURS

SERVES
6

1 vanilla bean
3 cups (750 mL) 15% cream
½ cup (125 mL) sugar
1 envelope + 1 tsp (5 mL) gelatin
3 Tbsp (45 mL) cold water
canola oil
3 cups (750 mL) strawberries,
*   quartered*
⅓ cup (75 mL) sugar
fresh mint leaves, to decorate

Slice vanilla bean in half, lengthwise. With tip of knife, scrape seeds from inside. In saucepan, place bean and seeds, cream and sugar. Simmer slowly for 5 minutes. Remove from heat and cool. Remove vanilla bean.

In bowl, let gelatin expand in cold water for 5 minutes. Add a little of warm vanilla cream to melt gelatin completely. Fold melted gelatin into cream mixture.

Lightly oil 6 ramekins with ½ cup (125 mL) capacity. Pour in vanilla cream mixture. Refrigerate for 6 hours.

In food processor, blend strawberries and sugar to make coulis.

Turn out each panna cotta onto a plate by placing bottom of ramekins into warm water and running knife around ramekin edges. Drizzle coulis around panna cotta and decorate with mint leaves.

Double-Lemon Pie

PREPARATION TIME
25 MINUTES

WAITING TIME
1 HOUR

COOKING TIME
55 MINUTES

SERVES
8

Pastry (Pie Crust)

¾ cup (175 mL) flour
¼ tsp (1 mL) salt
2 Tbsp (25 mL) brown sugar, packed
⅓ cup (75 mL) very cold unsalted
    butter, cut into pieces
1 Tbsp (15 mL) very cold
    shortening, cut into pieces
1 to 2 Tbsp (15 to 30 mL) iced water

Filling

2 lemons
2 limes
¾ cup (175 mL) sugar
3 Tbsp (45 mL) flour
2 eggs
¼ cup (50 mL) unsalted butter, melted

In food processor, mix flour, salt, and brown sugar. Add butter and shortening and process intermittently for a few seconds until mixture has granular texture. Add water and process until ball starts to form. Remove dough from processer and continue forming ball with your hands. Flour it and then wrap in plastic wrap. Refrigerate for 30 minutes.

Place rack on bottom level of oven. Preheat oven to 375°F (190°C).

Roll out pastry and place in bottom of a 9-inch (23-cm) springform pan. Refrigerate for 30 minutes. Prick pastry with fork and cover it with aluminum foil. Cover with dried peas and cook in oven for 25 minutes.

Filling

Finely grate 1 lemon and 1 lime for zest. Set aside. Juice citrus fruits and set aside.

In bowl, cream together sugar, flour and eggs until mixture is smooth and well mixed. Beat in butter, then zest and citrus juices.

Pour filling onto crust and bake in oven for about 30 minutes. If desired, brown pie under the broiler.

Remove pie from oven, cool and then refrigerate to cool completely before serving.

AS FOR WINE?

If you want to serve wine with this dessert, try a delicious Italian lemon liqueur, a Limoncello Di Leva.

Coffee Cake

Cake

2 tsp (10 mL) instant coffee
1 Tbsp (15 mL) hot water
¾ cup (175 mL) milk
¼ cup (50 mL) coffee or plain yogurt
3 cups (750 mL) pastry flour
1 Tbsp (15 mL) baking powder
1 tsp (5 mL) baking soda
1 cup (250 mL) unsalted butter,
  softened
1¾ cups (425 mL) sugar
1 Tbsp (15 mL) vanilla extract
5 eggs

Coffee Icing

2 Tbsp (25 mL) instant coffee
2 Tbsp (25 mL) hot water
1 cup (250 mL) sliced almonds
1½ cups (375 mL) unsalted
  butter, softened
4 cups (1 L) icing sugar

Cake

Dissolve instant coffee in hot water. Cool.

Place rack in centre of oven. Preheat oven to 350°F (180°C). Butter 2 round pans, 8 inches (20 cm) in diameter.

In small bowl, mix coffee, milk and yogurt. In another bowl, mix flour, baking powder and baking soda.

In a third bowl, using electric mixer, beat butter, sugar and vanilla until mixture becomes pale. Add eggs, one at a time, beating until well mixed.

Add dry ingredients and liquid ingredients to butter mixture, alternating between the two, and mix using wooden spoon.

Pour cake batter into two pans. Bake in oven for 35 to 40 minutes or until toothpick inserted in centre comes out clean. Cool cakes before turning out to cool on wire rack.

Coffee Icing

Dissolve instant coffee in hot water. Cool.

In skillet, toast sliced almonds. Set aside.

In bowl, beat butter, icing sugar and coffee until well mixed. Set aside.

Assembly

Slice each cake in half, horizontally. Set aside about 2 cups (500 mL) of icing for sides and top of cake. Spread remaining icing between each layer of cake. Ice sides and top, then cover with toasted almond slices.

WINE WITH DESSERT?

This cake is the perfect occasion to discover a Mavrodaphne, an amazing liqueur wine from Greece.

Apple and Pear
puff pastry pie

PREPARATION TIME
20 MINUTES

COOKING TIME
25 MINUTES

SERVES
4 TO 6

½ lb (250 g) store-bought puff
   pastry, thawed, cold
2 Tbsp (25 mL) milk
1 Tbsp (15 mL) sugar
3 red pears
water and lemon juice
1 cup (250 mL) pink applesauce
   (see note below)
¼ cup (50 mL) apricot jam, warm

Place rack on bottom level of oven. Preheat oven to 350°F (180°C).

Roll out puff pastry and cut to form a 9-inch (23-cm) square.

Using knife, carefully cut a ⅓-inch (1-cm) strip of pastry from each edge of the rolled puff pastry.

Brush edges of the pastry square with milk and attach the strips of pastry to the edges. Brush top of strip with milk and sprinkle with sugar.

Cut pears in half and remove rough core and seeds using melon baller. With a sharp knife, thinly slice pear halves. Immediately soak in water with drop or two of lemon juice in it.

Spread applesauce over pastry without touching edges. Lay pears on applesauce, overlapping one slice over another.

Bake in oven for about 25 minutes. Brush with warm apricot jam and serve.

You can buy pink applesauce or make it yourself. Just cook unpeeled apples, then pass them through a food mill. Very red apple varieties will make for a nice pink applesauce.

161

This recipe was invented to celebrate the birthday of Sébastien Benoît, host of CBC's "Des vertes et des pas mûres." Chocolate maniacs will die of pleasure.

Chocolate Cake

PREPARATION TIME
40 MINUTES

COOKING TIME
1 HOUR

SERVES
10 TO 12

Cake

2 cups (500 mL) pastry flour
1 cup (250 mL) cocoa
2 tsp (10 mL) baking powder
8 eggs, room temperature
1 tsp (5 mL) cream of tartar
3 cups (750 mL) sugar
1 cup (250 mL) vegetable oil
1 cup (250 mL) buttermilk
1 Tbsp (15 mL) vanilla extract

Syrup

½ cup (125 mL) sugar
¾ cup (175 mL) water

Chocolate Icing

1¼ cups (300 mL) unsalted
    butter, softened
¼ cup (50 mL) vegetable oil
¼ cup (50 mL) 35% whipping cream
5 cups (1.25 L) icing sugar
1 cup (250 mL) cocoa

Cake

Place rack in centre of oven. Preheat oven to 350°F (180°C).

Cover bottom of two 9-inch (23-cm) springform pans with parchment paper, then butter and flour pans.

In bowl, sift together flour, cocoa and baking powder. Set aside.

In another bowl, using an electric mixer at maximum speed, beat eggs, cream of tartar and sugar until mixture doubles in size, about 8 minutes. Add oil, buttermilk and vanilla. Reduce mixing speed, add dry ingredients, then mix rapidly.

Pour batter into cake pans. Bake in oven for about 1 hour or until toothpick inserted into the centre comes out clean. Cool cakes on wire rack. Cut each cake in half, horizontally, for icing.

Syrup

In saucepan, bring sugar and water to a boil.

Chocolate Icing

In bowl, beat together all ingredients until mixture becomes smooth.

First brush each layer of cake with syrup. Then spread icing on each layer. Assemble the two halves and finish by icing the cake completely.

WHAT TO DRINK?

A glass of milk
or a Late Bottle
Vintage (LBV)
Port wine.

Preparing a sabayon can be daunting. Truth is, you only need to have a good arm and to make sure that the mix doesn't cook for too long, so it doesn't turn into an omelette. Well assembled, a Sabayon isn't a fragile dessert. It can even be refrigerated for several hours in bowls without losing its volume or smoothness. I also use this Sabayon to make gratins when berries are in season. I cover the fruit with sabayon and broil for a few minutes in the oven to brown.

Maple Sabayon
with caramelized pears

PREPARATION TIME
10 MINUTES

COOKING TIME
20 MINUTES

SERVES
6

Caramelized Pears

3 Tbsp (45 mL) honey
2 Tbsp (25 mL) butter
6 pears, peeled, seeded and
    cut into 6 pieces

Maple Sabayon

6 egg yolks
½ cup (125 mL) maple syrup
¼ cup (50 mL) whisky

Caramelized Pears

In large skillet, heat honey and butter over high heat until mixture is golden. Add pears and cook about 4 minutes per side. Reduce heat if fruit cooks too quickly. Sauté until pears are golden. Set aside.

Maple Sabayon

In upper part of double boiler, before heating, beat egg yolks, maple syrup and whisky. Place upper part over simmering water and beat continuously for 8 to 10 minutes, until mixture is smooth and thick.

Place pears into 6 martini glasses and top with sabayon. Serve immediately.

WINE WITH THIS DESSERT?
Why not! Take advantage of the occasion to discover two beautiful dessert wines: a Recioto di Soave from Italy or a Coteaux du Layon from the Loire valley.

Sublime Coconut Cake

PREPARATION TIME
50 MINUTES

WAITING TIME
2 HOURS

COOKING TIME
1 HOUR

SERVES
10 TO 12

Cake

3 cups (750 mL) pastry flour
1 Tbsp (15 mL) baking powder
1¼ cups (300 mL) unsalted
    butter, softened
1 cup (250 mL) sugar
4 eggs
1½ cups (375 mL) milk

Coconut Garnish

2 cups (500 mL) sweetened
    concentrated milk
5 egg yolks, lightly beaten
¾ cup (175 mL) unsalted butter,
    softened
1½ cups (375 mL) roasted
    pecans, chopped
2 cups (500 mL) unsweetened
    coconut, grated (250 g bag)
2 tsp (10 mL) vanilla extract

Homemade Marshmallow

1½ cups (375 mL) sugar
⅓ cup (75 mL) hot water
1 tsp (5 mL) vanilla extract
4 tsp (20 mL) gelatin
½ cup (125 mL) cold water

Finishing Touch

1½ cups (375 mL) unsweetened
    coconut, in flakes or grated
    (see note below)

Cake

Place rack in centre of oven. Preheat oven to 350°F (180°C). Cover bottom of two 8-inch (20-cm) round cake pans with parchment paper and grease with butter.

In bowl, mix flour and baking powder. In another bowl, beat butter and sugar with electric mixer until mixture is white. Add eggs, one at a time, while beating. Delicately fold in milk and dry ingredients, alternating between wet and dry.

Pour batter into cake pans and bake in oven for 30 to 35 minutes, or until a toothpick inserted in centre comes out clean. Cool and turn out onto wire rack.

Coconut Garnish

In saucepan, before heating, beat concentrated milk, egg yolks and butter. Cook over low heat for 10 to 15 minutes, stirring with a wooden spoon. Take care not to boil. Add pecans, coconut and vanilla. Mix and cool for 2 hours in refrigerator.

Homemade Marshmallow

In bowl, mix sugar and hot water. Add vanilla. In another bowl, let gelatin expand in cold water for 2 to 3 minutes. Completely dissolve gelatin in microwave or using double boiler. Add gelatin to sugar mixture. Mix and cool. Beat with electric mixer for about 10 minutes, or until mixture has the texture of a soft meringue.

Assembly

Slice cakes in half, horizontally. Remove curved part of last (top) layer of cake. Spread one third of coconut garnish between each layer, then ice cake completely with homemade marshmallow. With your hands, gently cover the cake with coconut flakes. Keep the cake in a cool place, but not in the refrigerator.

To decorate this cake, we've used coconut flakes. Larger than grated coconut, they give the cake an airy, fluffy appearance. It looks like a feathered cake! It's the ideal dessert for a christening or small wedding. Coconut flakes are sold in bulk at natural food stores. If you can't find them, grated coconut will do. Leftover concentrated milk can be frozen.

When I was a food critic for the magazine *Elle Québec*, I'd often order Caramel Custard, my favourite dessert. This recipe, though simple, is ruined all too often; either it's not cooked right (air pockets spoil the texture) or there's not enough syrup. Even though it's a fragile dessert, when you succeed in making it, it's divine.

Caramel Custard

PREPARATION TIME
25 MINUTES

COOKING TIME
40 MINUTES

WAITING TIME
4 HOURS

SERVES
6

Caramel
½ cup (125 mL) sugar
2 Tbsp (25 mL) water

Custard
¼ cup (50 mL) sugar
2 tsp (10 mL) vanilla extract
2 cups (500 mL) warm milk
3 eggs

Place rack in centre of oven. Preheat oven to 350°F (180°C).

Caramel
In small or medium saucepan, heat sugar and water until a dark-coloured (mahogany) caramel is obtained. Divide caramel among 6 ramekins (½ cup / 125 mL capacity each). Cool.

Custard
Add sugar and vanilla to warm milk. Stir until sugar has dissolved completely. In bowl, beat eggs. Fold in hot liquid, while beating. Pour custard into ramekins.

Create double boiler by placing a cloth on bottom of a large ovenproof pan. Place ramekins on top of cloth and fill pan with hot water until water reaches halfway up ramekins. Cook in oven for about 40 minutes. Water must never boil.

Remove ramekins from oven and water. Cool in refrigerator for 4 hours.

Run a knife around edges of custard, turn over and serve very cold.

To add the finishing touch to a nice supper, I often serve small portions—much to the appreciation of my female guests—of crème brûlée in lovely spoons. To do this, put a little cooked crème brûlée, cooled, in soupspoons. Sprinkle with sugar and get ready for the show! To caramelize the sugar, turn on a stove element (coil or gas) and heat up the blades of two old knives, protecting your hand with an oven mitt. Slowly slide a hot knife blade across the sugar in front of your guests to melt down the sugar. Wow!

Crème Brûlée

PREPARATION TIME
15 MINUTES

COOKING TIME
40 MINUTES

WAITING TIME
4 HOURS

SERVES
4

2 ¼ cups (560 ml) 35% cream
1 vanilla bean or 1 tsp (5 mL)
vanilla extract
5 egg yolks
½ cup (125 mL) sugar

Place rack in centre of oven. Preheat oven to 325°F (170°C).

In saucepan, heat cream for 5 minutes with vanilla bean cut in half, without boiling, just enough to brew vanilla. Scrape out vanilla seeds and mix with cream. If you don't have a vanilla bean, add vanilla extract to the warm cream.

In bowl, beat egg yolks and half the sugar. Add warm cream, while stirring. Pour mixture into four crème brûlée moulds (¾ cup / 180 mL capacity) or ramekins.

Create double boiler by placing a cloth on bottom of a large ovenproof pan. Place ramekins on top of cloth and fill pan with hot water until water reaches halfway up ramekins. Cook in oven for about 35 minutes.

Cool and refrigerate until completely chilled, about 4 hours.

Sprinkle each crème brûlée with remaining sugar and caramelize quickly using a crème brûlée iron or torch. You may also caramelize crèmes brûlée under very high broil in oven. Serve immediately.

WHAT TO DRINK?
A Moscatel de Setubal
from Portugal.

Beet Cake

PREPARATION TIME
30 MINUTES

COOKING TIME
1 HOUR

SERVES
10 TO 12

3 cups (750 mL) pastry flour
1 Tbsp (15 mL) baking powder
1 tsp (5 mL) baking soda
2 tsp (10 mL) ground cinnamon
1 tsp (5 mL) ground nutmeg
1 cup (250 mL) pineapple, crushed,
    well drained
1 cup (250 mL) dates, pitted
    and chopped
1 cup (250 mL) dried raisins
1 cup (250 mL) chopped pecans
1 cup (250 mL) vegetable oil
1½ cups (375 mL) brown sugar, packed
4 eggs
2 cups (500 mL) beets, about
    2 medium, peeled and grated

Icing

¼ cup (60 mL) unsalted
    butter, softened
2 cups (500 mL) icing sugar
1 cup (250 mL) 35% whipping cream
½ tsp (2 mL) vanilla extract

Place rack in centre of oven. Preheat oven to 350°F (180°C). Butter and flour a 9-inch (23-cm) tube pan. The pan can have fluted sides.

In bowl, mix flour, baking powder, baking soda, cinnamon and nutmeg. Set aside.

In another bowl, mix pineapple, dates, raisins and pecans. Set aside.

In large bowl, beat vegetable oil and brown sugar with electric mixer until well mixed. Add eggs, one at a time, beating well between each addition, until mixture is smooth and creamy. Add grated beets. Fold dry ingredients into wet ingredients. Finish by folding in fruit and nut mixture.

Pour batter into pan. Bake in oven for about 1 hour or until toothpick comes out clean.

Cool for 10 minutes, then turn out onto a wire rack. Cool completely.

Icing

In bowl, beat butter and sugar for 1 minute. Add cream and vanilla extract and continue beating for 1 or 2 minutes until mixture is smooth and somewhat thick. Spread icing onto cake just before serving.

A cookbook without a brownie recipe isn't a cookbook. Some like them hot, others prefer them without nuts, and the reasonable make them without icing. No matter how you like them, they're a must. Mine are decadent, with chocolate *and* cream cheese frosting.

Brownies

PREPARATION TIME
25 MINUTES

COOKING TIME
40 MINUTES

SERVES
12

Cake

4 oz (100 g) unsweetened
    chocolate, chopped
4 oz (100 g) semi-sweet
    chocolate, chopped
1 cup (250 mL) unsalted butter,
    softened
1½ cups (375 mL) sugar
4 eggs, room temperature
1 Tbsp (15 mL) vanilla extract
1 cup (250 mL) flour
½ tsp (2 mL) baking powder
1 cup (250 mL) chopped
    pecans (optional)

Frosting

4 oz (100 g) semi-sweet chocolate
2 Tbsp (25 mL) unsalted butter
2 Tbsp (25 mL) water
4 oz (125 g) cream cheese, softened
1 cup (250 mL) icing sugar, sifted

Cake

Place rack in centre of oven. Preheat oven to 325°F (160°C). Butter a 13- × 9-inch (33- × 23-cm) pan.

Melt chocolate in double boiler, stirring. Set aside.

In bowl, beat butter and sugar with electric mixer. Add eggs, one at a time, and beat until mixture becomes pale and creamy. While beating, add melted chocolate and vanilla.

In another bowl, sift together flour and baking powder. Fold dry ingredients and pecans into chocolate mixture, using wooden spoon.

Pour brownie mixture into pan and bake in oven for about 40 minutes, or until cake edge of brownie is firm and crunchy. Cool in pan.

Frosting

In small saucepan, heat chocolate, butter and water over low heat until mixture is smooth. Set aside.

In bowl, beat cream cheese. Add chocolate mixture. While beating, gradually add icing sugar until frosting is smooth and well mixed.

Frost brownies evenly and cut into squares. If desired, serve with vanilla ice cream.

The recent trend in restaurants is this dessert, which is just a little chocolate cake that isn't quite cooked enough. All right, this fact detracts from the romanticism. A television viewer I met at the market gave me a super idea. He hides a large pitted cherry in the centre before cooking it … just like cherry blossoms! Why not a cherry soaked in alcohol? It's a very simple recipe. You can prepare it ahead of time, refrigerate it and cook it at the last minute. If refrigerated, it will need to cook for about 13 minutes for the centre to stay fudgy.

Chocolate Fudge Cakes

PREPARATION TIME
20 MINUTES

COOKING TIME
10 MINUTES

SERVES
6

3 eggs
2 egg yolks
3 Tbsp (45 mL) sugar
½ cup (125 mL) unsalted butter
4 oz (100 g) semi-sweet
    chocolate, chopped
⅓ cup (75 mL) flour

Place rack in centre of oven. Preheat oven to 375°F (190°C).

Butter well and sugar 6 ramekins (½ cup / 125 mL capacity).

In bowl, beat eggs, egg yolks and sugar for 5 minutes.

Melt butter in saucepan over very low heat. Add chocolate and stir until melted. Carefully fold into egg and sugar mixture. Fold in flour.

Divide equally among the ramekins and cook in oven for about 10 minutes.

Turn out immediately onto a plate. The centre of the cake should be creamy. Decorate with red berries and icing sugar.

AS FOR WINE?
A Banyuls
or a Maury.

175

Not so long ago, we used to offer maple syrup as a gift to the French. I now prefer to give ice cider, and it's always a great hit. The Americans, Italians and Japanese are all fascinated by this Québec product, unique to our climate. I hope this liqueur-like cider is protected from cheap imposters.

Ice Cider Jelly

PREPARATION TIME
10 MINUTES

REFRIGERATION
3 HOURS, 30 MINUTES

COOKING TIME
2 MINUTES

SERVES
6

1 tsp (5 mL) gelatin
¾ cup + 2 Tbsp (210 mL)
*   apple juice, cold*
½ cup (125 mL) ice cider
18 fresh raspberries
½ cup (125 mL) 35% whipping cream
1 Tbsp (15 mL) sugar

In bowl, mix gelatin and apple juice. Let gelatin expand for 5 minutes and then dissolve in microwave oven. Add gelatin to ice cider and mix well.

Divide mixture among 6 small decorative or martini glasses. Refrigerate for about 1 hour and a half or until jelly is firm enough to suspend raspberry in it. Insert 3 raspberries into each glass of jelly. Return glasses to refrigerator for about 2 hours.

Using an electric mixer, beat cream and sugar together until soft peaks form.

Dollop some whipped cream onto ice cider jelly. Serve before dessert.

While the European recipe inspires my version of tarte Tatin, I've given it a New World twist by adding caramel and pecans. I make this recipe so that it comes out of the oven about 15 minutes after my friends have arrived. I turn it out before their eyes, they drool over it until dessert … and I'm jubilant.

Tarte Tatin
with pears and pecans

PREPARATION TIME
20 MINUTES

COOKING TIME
40 MINUTES

COOLING TIME
1 HOUR

SERVES
8

Pastry (for 2 pie crusts)*

1¾ cups (450 mL) flour
½ tsp (2 mL) salt
10 Tbsp (150 mL) very cold unsalted
    butter, cut into pieces
2 Tbsp (25 mL) very cold
    shortening, cut into pieces
¼ to ⅓ cup (50 to 75 mL)
    ice-cold water

Filling

5 firm pears, peeled, cut in
    half and seeded
2 Tbsp (25 mL) unsalted butter
⅓ cup (75 mL) brown sugar
½ cup (125 mL) roasted pecans,
    halved

Pastry
Process flour and salt for a few seconds in food processor.

Add butter and shortening and process intermittently for a few seconds until mixture has granular texture. Add water and process until ball starts to form. Remove dough from processor and continue forming ball with your hands. Flour it and then wrap in plastic wrap. Refrigerate dough for about 1 hour.

Place rack on bottom level of oven.
Preheat oven to 350°F (180°C).

Filling
In ovenproof 8-inch (20-cm) skillet, caramelize pears on all sides in butter and brown sugar. Take care, however, as the more they cook, the more fragile they'll become. Add pecans and mix well. Arrange pears with rounded sides down in skillet. Remove skillet from heat and set aside.

Roll out half of dough to form circle slightly larger than skillet diameter. Place dough over pears. Tuck in edges of dough between pears and side of skillet. Bake in oven for about 30 minutes.

Let stand for 5 minutes. Turn out onto plate and serve immediately.

*Carefully wrap the second half of the dough with plastic wrap and freeze it for later use. Thaw in refrigerator.

Since this dessert has to be prepared at the last minute, it's perfect for a break after the main course. I often prepare it in front of my friends, who love to help. This is a visual surprise, and oh so good!

Choco-Espresso Risotto

PREPARATION TIME
15 MINUTES

COOKING TIME
25 MINUTES

SERVES
4 TO 5

½ cup (125 mL) arborio
    or carnaroli rice
3 Tbsp (45 mL) unsalted butter
3 Tbsp (45 mL) Grand Marnier
    or other orange liqueur
2 Tbsp (25 mL) espresso or strong
    coffee
3 cups (750 mL) milk, warm
¼ cup (50 mL) 35% whipping cream
3 oz (75 g) white chocolate, chopped
2 oz (50 g) milk or dark
    chocolate, chopped

In medium-large saucepan, brown rice in butter over medium heat.

Add orange liqueur and reduce by half, stirring at the same time.

Pour the warm milk in a large measuring cup. Add espresso to warm milk. Add ½ cup (125 mL) of the milk mixture to the rice. Cook over medium heat, stirring from time to time, until liquid is almost completely absorbed. Repeat steps. This should take about 20 minutes. At that point, liquid should be completely absorbed and rice should be tender.

Add cream and chocolate. Don't stir too much in order to maintain marbled effect of chocolate.

Serve this risotto in espresso coffee cups. Top with whipped cream if you like.

Every family in Québec has its sugar pie recipe. This pie is exactly like the one my mother used to make. When my friend Pascal came over to my house, we'd run off with the pie and two spoons.

Sugar Pie

PREPARATION TIME
5 MINUTES

COOKING TIME
30 MINUTES

SERVES
6 TO 8

1¼ cups (300 mL) brown sugar
2 Tbsp (25 mL) cornstarch
2 Tbsp (25 mL) flour
1 cup (250 mL) 35% whipping cream
1 egg
2 tsp (10 mL) vanilla extract
1 pie crust, uncooked
    (see recipe on page 179)

Place rack on bottom level of oven. Preheat oven to 375°F (190°C).

In saucepan, before heating, combine brown sugar and cornstarch. Add remaining ingredients and mix well.

Cook over medium heat until boiling and thick. Pour into pie crust and bake in oven, about 25 minutes.

Cake with Pecan Praline

Cake

2 cups (500 mL) pastry flour
2 tsp (10 mL) baking powder
¾ cup (175 mL) unsalted
    butter, softened
¾ cup (175 mL) sugar
1 tsp (5 mL) vanilla extract
4 eggs
¾ cup (175 mL) milk

Syrup

3 Tbsp (45 mL) water
1 Tbsp (15 mL) rum
¼ cup (50 mL) sugar

Pecan Praline

2 ½ cups (625 mL) pecans
1 egg white, lightly beaten
¾ cup (175 mL) brown sugar

Maple Icing

4 cups (1 L) icing sugar
1 cup (250 mL) unsalted
    butter, softened
½ cup (125 mL) maple syrup

Cake

Place rack in centre of oven. Preheat oven to 350°F (180°C). Cover bottom of two 8-inch (20-cm) square cake pans with parchment paper. Butter both sides of paper.

In bowl, mix flour and baking powder. In another bowl, beat butter, sugar and vanilla using electric mixer until mixture is pale. Add eggs, one at a time, beating at the same time. Add dry ingredients and milk, alternating. Mix with electric mixer. Spread mixture into cake pans.

Bake in oven for about 20 minutes or until toothpick inserted in centre comes out clean. Turn out and cool on wire rack.

Syrup

In small saucepan, bring all ingredients to a boil and simmer for 1 minute. Remove from heat and cool.

Pecan Praline

Preheat oven to 400°F (200°C). Dip pecans into egg white and then coat generously with brown sugar. Place on two cookie sheets covered with parchment paper. Leave enough space between pecans to prevent them from touching during cooking. Cook in oven for about 10 minutes. Cool and chop coarsely. Set aside one third of pecans to decorate cake top.

Maple Icing

In bowl, beat icing sugar, butter and maple syrup with electric mixer until smooth. Reserve one third of icing for cake top. Fold two thirds of pecans in remaining icing.

Assembly

Cut each cake in half, horizontally. Place a cake layer flat on serving plate. Cover with one third of syrup, then continue with one quarter of icing. Repeat steps with other two cake layers. Spread reserved icing onto last cake layer and top with reserved pecans, pressing lightly with hands.

A LITTLE WINE?
A good Tawny
Port wine.

Black Forest Cake

Cake

1¾ cups (430 mL) pastry flour
½ cup (125 mL) cocoa
1 tsp (5 mL) baking powder
½ cup (125 mL) unsalted butter,
    softened
1¼ cups (310 mL) sugar
2 eggs
1 tsp (5 mL) vanilla extract
1 cup (250 mL) milk

Garnish

one 19-oz (540-mL) jar of
    morello cherries, drained
½ cup (125 mL) sugar
3 Tbsp (45 mL) kirsch
large chocolate shavings

Chantilly Cream

3 cups (750 mL) 35% whipping cream
½ cup (125 mL) sugar
2 tsp (10 mL) vanilla extract

Cake

Place rack in centre of oven. Preheat
oven to 350°F (180°C).

Cover 2 round pans (8 inches / 20 cm) with
parchment paper and butter well.

In bowl, sift flour, cocoa and baking powder. Set aside.

In another bowl, using electric mixer, beat
butter and sugar until mixture is smooth. Add
eggs and vanilla. Mix well. Add dry ingredients,
alternating with milk. Spread into cake pans.

Cook in oven for about 30 minutes or until
toothpick inserted in centre comes out clean.

Cool slightly and turn out. Cool completely on wire rack.

Garnish

Drain cherries and set aside ½ cup (125 mL)
of their juice. In small saucepan, bring juice
and sugar to a boil. Once sugar is dissolved,
add kirsch and remove from heat. Cool.

Chantilly Cream

In bowl, beat cream, sugar and vanilla
until peaks form.

Assembly

Cut cakes in half, horizontally. Place one layer
on serving plate. Top with one quarter of the
cherry syrup, using spoon. Continue with one
quarter of Chantilly Cream and half of cherries.
Cover with second cake layer. Top with one
quarter of syrup and continue with one quarter
of Chantilly Cream. Cover with third cake layer,
one quarter of syrup, one quarter of Chantilly
Cream and remaining cherries. Cover with last
cake layer, pour remaining syrup on top,
then cover with remaining Chantilly Cream.
Garnish with chocolate shavings.

**WINE FOR DESSERT
... WHY NOT?**

Port wine and
chocolate go
well together.
This cake will be
delicious with a
Late Bottle Vintage
(LBV) Port wine
or with a Banyuls.
This dessert
wine from
Languedoc-Roussillon
harmonizes well
with chocolate.

Cheese Trilogy

Warm Goat Cheese on Apple

PREPARATION TIME **5 MINUTES**

COOKING TIME **7 MINUTES**

SERVES **6**

1 red apple
1 Tbsp (15 mL) walnut oil
one 3⅓-oz (100-g) roll of
    fresh goat cheese,
    cut into 6 slices
2 Tbsp (25 mL) hazelnuts,
    chopped
Fleur de sel
Freshly ground pepper
1½ tsp (7.5 mL) honey
1½ tsp (7.5 mL) fresh
    chives, minced

Place rack on top level of
oven. Preheat oven to broil.

Cut both ends of apple and
then cut it into six round slices.
With the tip of a knife, remove
centre of each slice. Place onto
cookie sheet and brush with oil.

Cook apples under broil for about
5 minutes.

Place a piece of cheese on each
slice of apple. Sprinkle with
hazelnuts. Cook in oven for 1 to 2
minutes until cheese starts to melt.

After removing from oven, sprinkle
with a pinch of salt and season
with pepper. Drizzle honey on top.
Sprinkle with chives. Serve warm.

Brie and Pistachio "Candies"

PREPARATION TIME **15 MINUTES**

COOKING TIME **15 MINUTES**

SERVES **12**

3 shallots, finely chopped
2 Tbsp (25 mL) butter
2 phyllo sheets
¼ cup (50 mL) butter, melted
¼ cup (50 mL) pistachios, crushed
2 oz (60 g) brie, rind removed,
    cubed into ½ inch (1 cm)
    pieces

Place rack in centre of oven.
Preheat oven to 350°F (180°C).

In saucepan, soften shallots
in butter.

Place a phyllo sheet on work
surface and brush with melted
butter. Sprinkle with pistachios
and cover with second phyllo
sheet. Cut into 12 squares
of 4 inches (10 cm) each.

In middle of each square, place
piece of cheese and 1 tsp (5 mL)
of the shallots. Roll square on
itself and pinch pastry on
each end of cheese to give
it the shape of candy.

Brush with butter and place on
cookie sheet. Cook in oven for
about 15 minutes. Serve warm.

Crème Brûlée with Blue Cheese

PREPARATION TIME **5 MINUTES**

COOKING TIME **15 MINUTES**

SERVES **10**

1 cup (250 mL) 35% cream
⅓ cup (75 mL) blue cheese,
    crumbled
5 egg yolks
salt and pepper
2 Tbsp (25 mL) finely chopped
    roasted walnuts, approximately

Place rack in centre of oven.
Preheat oven to 300°F (150°C).

In saucepan, slowly heat cream
and cheese until melted.
Remove from heat. Cool.

Place egg yolks in bowl. Add cheese
mixture while beating. Season
with salt and pepper. Pour into 10
ramekins (¼ cup / 60 mL each).

Place ramekins in ovenproof
pan and fill with hot water
halfway up ramekins. Cook
in oven for about 15 minutes.
Refrigerate for 3 to 4 hours.

Sprinkle with walnuts and serve.

"We're almost done,
          Beatrice."